"Young's story of family, survival, faith and hope [maps] the path for others to find their way to beautiful."

—*The San Diego Union-Tribune*

"*On Our Way to Beautiful* is filled with humor and insight."

—*The* (New Orleans) *Times-Picayune Book Review*

"Young shares . . . her determination to escape the poverty in her community and the cultural traditions of 'doing what had always been done.'" —*Richmond Times-Dispatch*

"A touching tribute . . . like listening to the narrator on *The Wonder Years* or *The Waltons*—a soothing voice that reads between the lines. . . . It takes great skill to tell a life's story in so short a space."

—*Fort Worth Star-Telegram*

"Yolanda learns about all kinds of love from her family: The love between a man and a woman [and] the love between a mother and her son." —*Black Issues Book Review*

PHOTO: © CARL POSEY

YOLANDA YOUNG graduated from Howard University and the Georgetown University Law Center. Her work has appeared in *USA Today* and *Essence* magazine. In 2002 she was selected to participate in the PEN/Faulkner Writers in Schools program and won a Mayor's Arts Award, presented by the Washington, D.C., Commission on Arts and Humanities. She is a Sunday school teacher at the Metropolitan Baptist Church in Washington. In the summer months she finds refuge in baseball parks, and during the winter, anyplace warm. To learn more, visit www.onourwaytobeautiful.com.

On Our Way
to Beautiful

RANDOM HOUSE TRADE PAPERBACKS / NEW YORK

On Our Way to Beautiful

A FAMILY MEMOIR

Yolanda Young

Library of Congress Cataloging-in-Publication Data
Young, Yolanda.
On our way to beautiful: a family memoir / Yolanda Young.
p.   cm.
ISBN 0-8129-6674-0
1. Young, Yolanda, 1968–   2. Young, Yolanda, 1968–   Family.   3. African American
women–Louisiana–Shreveport–Biography.   4. African American families–Louisiana–
Shreveport–Biography.   5. African Americans–Louisiana–Shreveport–Social life and
customs–20th century.   6. Shreveport (La.)–Biography.   7. Shreveport (La.)–Social life
and customs–20th century.   I. Title.
F379.S4 Y68 2002
976.3'99063'092–dc21   2001049244

Random House website address: www.atrandom.com
Printed in the United States of America
2 4 6 8 9 7 5 3 1

Book design by Victoria Wong

To my brother, Sededric O'Neal, my nephew, Jamaria,
and my first cousins, William, Benitris, Odell, Jr.,
Ardell, Dwayne, Derek, Donald, Jr., Michelle, Desmond,
Jamarcus, Meagan, and especially Donna, who
inspired this book. I pray we continue our parents'
legacy and always love one another.

Acknowledgments

Huge kisses for my earthly angels—my agent, Joanna Pulcini, and my first editor, Courtney Hodell. This book exists because of your patience and wisdom. Lois Smith Brady, I am forever in your debt for leading me to them. Thank you, Bruce Tracy, for the care and attention you and your team, especially Melody Guy, have given this project. Warm hugs for Linda Chester and my friends at her agency—Kelli, Gary, Liza, Cristi, and Anna. Thank you all for championing this book.

My thanks to the Sanders brothers, David and Adam, who from the very beginning encouraged me. My deepest gratitude to James Brathwaite, Sam McLemore, and Wilfred "Uncle B" Delphin for providing an ear, a shoulder, and, when it became necessary, a place to write. Then there were the early (and I'm sure) laborious chapter readings by my good friends: Candi and Joseph Carter; Reeves Carter and his wife, Karla; Father John Raphael; Erika Mobley; Kimberly Yates; Carlee McCullough; Eric Stroud; the Christophes—Angie, Mary, and Farrell; Susan Bronston Sullivan; Regina Davis; Charisse Williams; Tamu Wright; Wilbert Pryor; Kelli Doss; Jonah Edelman; Dwight and

Cecilia Jones; Mark Bolding; Shawn Bailey Williams; and Don Gibbs. And finally, my sincere thanks to Carranza Pryor for reading the whole kit and caboodle.

There are many people and institutions who came to my aid in the form of instruction, research, and funding. They are Dr. Willie Burton, author of *The Black Side of Shreveport,* Munson Steed and Randy Fling of *Rolling Out Magazine,* the National Newspaper Publishers Association, *The Shreveport Sun,* the D.C. Commission on the Arts and Humanities, the Martin Luther King Jr. Memorial Library, the Shreve Memorial Library, Washington Independent Writers, and the Writer's Center in Bethesda, Maryland. And I can't forget William O'Sullivan, Richard Peabody, and Paul Lisipky.

Finally, I extend all my heart to my great family. Your unfailing love and support continue to lift me. Thank you for trusting me with our story.

Contents

On Our Way
to Beautiful

On Our Way to Beautiful

When men began to increase in number on the earth and
daughters were born to them, the sons of God saw that the
daughters of men were beautiful . . . then the Lord said, My
spirit shall not always strive with man, for he also is flesh.

—*Genesis 6:1–3*

Once a year I make the drive back to my hometown of Shreveport, Louisiana. My journey begins as the sun rises over our na-
tion's capital. Before long I'm moving through smaller cities
that claim tobacco and the Confederate flag as symbols of
pride, wondering how long it will be before the smell of factory
smoke is replaced by the fertile aroma of livestock and chicken
flocks. Then the narrow roads begin to unwind—hugged on either side by pastures, cows, horses, and shacks—and so too
does my mind. As I ramble down bumpy paths, I stumble over
the memory of a day spent fishing in a nearby bayou with my
uncles, and the familiar smells of rank armpits and beer over-
whelm my senses. Later, I see shiny pumps and a black veil
waiting on top of an aging quilt and hear children running in
bare feet.

A tin of peanut brittle spotted at the counter of a country gas station lands my mind on my great-grandmother because that was her favorite candy. Big Momma was part of a chorus of tabernacle women who mothered me. She always said Shreveport was known as the city of churches because they sprout up on corners like strawberries in July. Word has it that there are more churches in my hometown than in any other city in the country. Hymns flow from their doors on Sunday mornings, while during the week the smiling church ladies greet you with words of encouragement as they skirt around the vestibule like bees on a honeycomb. "Baaaby, that was a fine prayer you did Sunday," Mrs. Davis would say as I walked by. "Whose girl is dat with you? Bring her next Sunday."

But as is the case with all of Louisiana, our little city wobbles between extremes. Our local dishes of gumbo, catfish, and dirty rice must be spicy hot. Juke joints squat next to churches, and betting slips compete with offering envelopes. Fire-and-brimstone ministers point out that we drink and gamble too much. That is, until one in their congregation "hits." Then it's time to bring a tithe of the winnings to the altar. All of this is summed up neatly by the two billboards I notice as I cross the Texas Street Bridge into my city's fold. One beckons you toward the HORSESHOE CASINO STRAIGHT AHEAD. Opposite, another shouts, WANNA WIN THE JACKPOT? COME TO JESUS. There is always the question of which road to take.

To enter Shreveport's downtown, travelers must cross our beloved Red River, which curls like a large garden snake around the city. The river is yet another contradiction. It does not remotely resemble the liquid silver color of the Mississippi. Instead, it pours out a murky clay red and flows as thick as soft mud across Louisiana. The only time it sparkles is at night, when the casino riverboats' carnival lights illuminate the city.

Following the curve of the river, crouched along the road leaving downtown, rests a neighborhood of little shacks that belie a city of over a quarter million. We call the houses shotgun because a bullet fired through the front entrance will pass through every room in the house before exiting the back door. It is a place where the children play dodgeball in the street but know to watch their manners, and every woman worth her salt can make a meal out of meat drippings, flour, eggs, and rice. The unpaved streets are filled with stray dogs, and after a rain the air smells like wet earth. On warm mornings, plump older women wearing blinding white maid uniforms congregate on corners and talk while awaiting the arrival of little blue buses that will take them to the homes where they work.

"Child, Pastor Green liked to got the church on fire Sunday, didn't he?"

"Yeah, girl, and did you hear Mrs. Rogers shouting in the back? You know that boy of hers keeps her on her knees. He ain't got good sense."

"Folks say what they want about her whiskey habit. That woman will give you the shirt off her back. That's how I know she close to God."

That neighborhood was called Stoner Hill. I grew up listening to the women there. Everyone in that phalanx had a family church, and most believed in God and agreed that it was through Jesus Christ that we all gained salvation. Growing up, I don't recall ever meeting someone who didn't have a faith—at least no one who would admit such a thing out loud. It was a place where all doctrine was respected; even door-knocking Jehovah's Witnesses were given the opportunity to speak their piece. Yes, Shreveport was the kind of city where everyone had a church, temple, or chapel they considered theirs, even if they'd only seen it from the inside a dozen times. A child from Stoner

Hill seldom made it out of puberty without a distant cousin or a neighbor dragging the youngster off to recite New Testament Scripture in the Easter pageant or sing carols in the Christmas program, blessing the child with at least a C.M.E. membership: attendance at Christmas, Mother's Day, and Easter.

I've been reciting Bible verses since I was old enough to say, "Jesus wept." My great-grandmother, Big Momma, used to say about the Bible, "Baby, you can find a word to carry you through anythang." Still, my very religious family managed to pick and choose which Scriptures to live by. The men would pray up a miracle in the deacons' corner and then enjoy a strong glass or two of Jack Daniel's after church. The women sang in the choir but cursed like sailors when their team fumbled on *Monday Night Football*. "I could pull up my skirt and beat that sorry-ass receiver to the ball," Big Momma would shout from the kitchen while stacking freshly washed dishes in cabinets.

I spent most of my childhood summers down the road from home at Big Momma's house. We began each day with the morning ritual she referred to as her labor of love—combing my hair. I would sit on the porch floor with my feet swinging over its edge while my head bobbed back and forth between Big Momma's legs as she tugged, parted, and braided my long, thick, nappy hair. Big Momma always sat perfectly upright, sucking in her breath with each drag of the comb, then releasing the air from her hollow Cherokee cheeks, never once bending her back. After she finished the job, she'd pat me on my head and say, "Now you beautiful." I'd rush to the bathroom, stand on the toilet seat, and peer over the sink into the mirror, eager to view this new and beautiful me. Of course, she never materialized. All I ever saw was my chubby face with a crown of lopsided plaits and a mouth full of what my momma teasingly called "beaver teeth" because they looked large enough to saw wood.

Besides our grooming, Big Momma and her band of swearing sopranos made sure their offspring got a proper Christian upbringing. Every Sunday there was morning church school and Baptist Training Union. And for one week every August the young ones were herded to Grambling, Louisiana, a small college town, for a gigantic statewide revival called Youth-En-Camp. Although the drive took only a few hours, it had the feel of a great adventure. This was due in part to the parcel of sheets, dresses, and fried chicken that always accompanied me but also because the decreased supervision allowed me to experience free will. It was during one of these revivals that I became hopeful that I would one day look into the mirror and see beauty in myself.

I was thirteen at the time—too old to be in one of the crayon classrooms but still too awkward to be cool. Before that summer I'd never thought that I could be beautiful—perhaps cute, on a good day, but never glamorous, radiant, or enchanting. Of course, up to that point, the only form of beauty I knew to desire was physical splendor, in which category I was sorely lacking. I was the tallest girl in my eighth-grade class, and when I tried to walk in dress shoes, my heels would slide out, causing me to trip over myself. Naturally, my only concern was ridding myself of awkwardness. Beauty was something I saw only in others. A woman's even-colored skin and bright white teeth made her beautiful, never the inner peace that sparkled in her eyes. I greatly admired the little girl's sunny Easter dress, adorned with white bows and ribbons, but gave no thought to the mother—needle in one hand, iron in the other, creating this lovely vision. And Big Momma's front lawn with its velvet violets, deep purple grape suckers, and yellow sunflowers floating in the air like balloons was beautiful, but never once did I consider the care they were given even as the flowers' first petals danced indiscriminately in the sunlight. I had always focused on my plainness, and it was this sorry image of myself that I took with me to Youth-En-Camp that summer. Only later would I understand that real beauty emanates from the heart.

At camp that summer, our daily activities started with 5 A.M. prayer and devotion, during which I often volunteered to pray out loud so that everyone could hear my conversation with God. Somewhere along the way I got the notion that you were the biggest coward and hypocrite if you didn't want to pray out loud. That to me suggested you were ashamed of the Lord, and even with all my insecurities and teenage angst, I wanted to be bigger than that. After breakfast, there was Bible-study class, lunch, and midday worship. There teenagers would offer testimonials, and thanks to those I referred to as our "holy staples" (they seemed as necessary to our religious experience as the flour and canned goods that lined the shelves of our neighborhood general store)—the girl who'd been suffering from multiple sclerosis who was walking for the first time in five years and the boys who overnight had been called to preach—the standard for godliness was set high.

Following dinner and church service came the dating game, which commenced on a dusty bridge that stretched a half mile long and linked Grambling to the town of Ruston. As a symbolic gesture, the bridge was closed while the campers lined up at its foot, over a thousand of us girls on the right while the boys, far fewer in number, stood on the left. Once we were all settled down, the boys would cross the street and become like ants sifting through a mound of brown sugar, seeking the perfect young lady to escort to the other side of the bridge for evening service at Rocky Valley Baptist Church. I was always with the leftover girls, and we would trail behind the couples, walking with our heads down, kicking at stones in the street.

Once the service got going, some of the girls would pretend to catch the Holy Spirit, which in our crowd of excitable teenagers was accompanied by a chorus of high-pitched screams, a tossing of hands, body tremors, and an uncontrollable desire to run up and down the aisles. A boy would then come to the rescue of his chosen damsel. In a coy attempt to contain her, the young man would often hold her down while reaching under her dress and squeezing her butt. I couldn't wait to be one of those high school girls who in a frenzy got to kick off my black patent-leather Nina sling-backs and get my butt squished by a handsome preacher boy. This would happen with several couples without fail year after year, and every time, after a few days of camp, our chaperones would realize that what raged within us was induced more by hormones than by the Holy Spirit.

Everyone knew the routine. Within three days of such free-for-all, an announcement would move our 11 P.M. curfew to 9:30. Dorm counselors would distribute leaflets listing the hazards (both spiritual and otherwise) of teen promiscuity. The boys and girls would no longer be allowed to couple but would instead have to sit on separate sides of the auditorium during all services. Then all this would culminate in a stern lecture on the sacredness of our bodies and the proper behavior one should exhibit in an Assembly of God.

That particular summer, however, our new director, Reverend Frank, tried a different approach. The minister was in his twenties and wore his youth on his sleeve. His shoes were always the exact color of his suits, whether burgundy, green, or mustard yellow. His hair was done up in glycerin curls that hung down the back of his neck. The day he came forward to address our behavior, he knew he didn't need to holler and spit because his carriage and deportment had already captured our attention. That fact was obvious from the way our eyes followed him reverently as he moved to the center of the pulpit. Once in position, he leaned over the podium, pulled up his suit sleeves, and tapped his foot on the floor. His eyes moved about the room dramatically. Then he stood still until the only sound filtering the air was the hum of his breath over the microphone. After clearing his throat, he began to read from Genesis in a deep voice that made every syllable resonate.

When men began to increase in number on the earth and daughters were born to them, the sons of God saw that the daughters of men were beau-ti-fulll . . .

He snapped his neck up, startling us. Then he rocked his head back and asked in a teasing way, "Y'all having a good time? Y'all having fun yet? Young ladies, y'all looking good in those Calvins, ain't they, boys?"

"Yeah," the boys said, smiling broadly.

"I can't believe they are able to wear them even tighter than they did last summer. I know you fellas can barely keep your eyes in your head. Y'all acting just like the fellas did in Noah's day." Everybody looked around, not quite sure where he was going. "Why y'all looking at me funny? Did you think you invented the super freak? Shoot, women been fine and men been looking since Adam took a bite out of that apple." We fell over ourselves laughing. "Ain't nothin' wrong with that either . . . until you start getting carried away. Then, like God did with the flood, I gotta rein you back in."

Again Reverend Frank took a serious look at the Word.

And the Lord said, My spirit shall not always strive with man, for he also is flesh . . .

"See," he said, playful again, "those men were like you boys. They were like, 'I gotta have me some of that.' " Then, after taking stock of the assemblage, he yelled out, "Hey, which one of you fellas got the most phone numbers? Come on, I know y'all keeping score. Rodney," the reverend shouted out at a tall boy with eyebrows so thick they almost touched, "how many numbers you got?"

"Not too many, Rev," the boy said, looking as though he'd been caught with his hand going up a girl's skirt. A boy sitting next to him chimed in, "He's got over forty last we checked, Rev."

"Now, don't y'all wonder what Rodney or anybody is gon' do with forty phone numbers in one week's time? You know, it's a funny thing about sin and the flesh—they feed off of each other. They're like lined-up dominoes. When one falls, so go the others. That's what happened to Noah's posse." By speaking to us in our own language, Reverend Frank tightened his grip on our consciousness. He stared back at us gravely before continuing to read.

The earth was corrupt before God, and filled with violence; for all flesh had corrupted his way upon the earth.

"They weren't just lusting after women either," Reverend Frank said with a finger in the air. "The men competed for the biggest boat to get around in, the flashiest cave to call home. They started lying on each other, being jealous of their fine women, and wanting what the other man had. They forgot all about God and the good that he put us here to do. And what do you think God did? He got mad, just like we did with y'all earlier this week." Back to his Bible he went.

Noah found grace in the eyes of the Lord. Noah was a just man and perfect in his generations, and Noah walked with God.

"Now, girls, here's something y'all can shout about. No matter what we've done in the past, God is always looking for the beautiful among us." Leaning closer toward us, he asked, "Why y'all still looking at me funny? Y'all still don't get what I'm trying to say? See, those folk were beautiful on the outside, but on the inside they were busy starting a whole lot of confusion, all but Noah with his old, beat-up, half-blind self. Noah was six hundred years old, so you know he had to be plenty ugly. But Noah was the one in whose eyes God saw beauty. 'Why?' you ask. Because Noah was the one searching himself. Noah was the one listening to the instruction of the spirit of God that dwells within each of us. You see, Noah knew what y'all need to get hip to."

Reverend Frank stooped and fanned his hands from his lavender shoes up to his matching jacket collar. "All of this is going to fade away, and all you'll be left with are the drops of grace you've left in your path. The day you can look in the mirror and say to yourself, 'Yesterday I did the best I could and today I'll do better than that,' is the day you'll see beauty in your eyes."

Reverend Frank walked to the edge of the stage. With each of his steps, our bodies grew heavier, sinking deeper into the red pew cushions. "You see, young people, we have the power to transform ourselves." He clasped his hands together and pulled them into his chest as though he was pleading with us. "Do this for me," he said slowly, in a somber voice. "Close your eyes and picture the most beautiful thing you've ever seen." I closed my eyes and saw Big Momma's front yard and the wildly sprinkled violets that she nourished with water long before anything pretty ever emerged from the ground. "It may be a pretty face you're seeing, but more than likely it's not. It may be something as small as a ladybug crawling up your arm or as grand as the

Christmas lights that hang across Natchitoches during the holidays, but it's something that leaves you filled with a blessedness."

Reverend Frank seemed to shuffle with his thoughts for a moment before continuing. "Let me show it to you another way. Think of a time when you've felt beautiful. Not pretty or admired, but when you were filled with happiness, optimism, and thanksgiving. Picture in your mind's eye the last time you felt safe, at home in yourself."

I didn't have to think back far. I would never have thought to call it such, but this feeling of beauty had come over me just a few months earlier when our family had gathered together for a Sunday celebration. Big Momma had sat in the center of a long banquet table. Flanking her were my sweet-faced grandmother and Momma. Forming an arch around them were my grandfather and many of my aunts and uncles. I sat sprinkled amongst them with all the other children, listening to our parents reflect on the many tragedies they'd endured and the things from which our family had been delivered. As the stories piled up, they all seemed to be saying what I felt at that moment—that every sadness is made bearable and every victory that much sweeter because we shared it all with one another. Among them I felt loved, complete, and safe.

When I opened my eyes, I saw the church with blurred vision. I didn't look around but knew that everyone around me was crying too. Reverend Frank's sermon had touched us like none we'd heard before. During most scoldings from the pulpit, we'd become disinterested stones listening to lectures that perplexed us as much as the story of Hesiod's *Creation*. But when Reverend Frank sat down, we were silent, still drinking his words. Over the years, their meaning seeped into my heart slowly, like rain into the ground. I have come to understand the many levels of beauty, the core of which for me is home, where my family nurtured the beauty in me the way Big Momma cherished her flowers. Before the spring tickled the buds, Big Momma was filled with anticipation. When her violets blossomed with an intensity that outshone anything her garden had produced the year before, she would clasp her hands together and pull them into her chest much the way Reverend Frank had. "Look a' 'dem, Londa," she would say, gazing out over her flowers. "Lord, they beautiful."

Hers was the beauty in the order of life. The fecund glory of her garden was all the sweeter because of its tenacious place in God's creation. When the days got shorter and the swelling pears and figs thudded to the ground, she knew, as I came to, that they would all rise again come spring like the next generation. It was the inevitability of that return, not the flowers and fruits themselves, that infused Big Momma's faith, and so it was with my gap-toothed beauty. She knew that our family had already planted the seeds—of mistakes, triumphs, and, most important, love. So she could see the hope in a little girl's smile and know that with her wise ministration it would endure through the seasons ahead.

Juneteenth

> In spite of this, you did not trust in the Lord your God,
> who went ahead of you on your journey, in fire by night and in
> a cloud by day, to search out places for you to camp and
> to show you the way you should go.
>
> —*Deuteronomy 1:32–33*

Big Momma always seemed in perpetual motion—walking or talking or both. On days when she had her strength, she would braid her thin hair that she hadn't cut in seven decades into two long ropes, and we would walk through the city bringing fresh ivy plants to her good friends in hospitals and nursing homes or, sometimes, to funeral parlors, Big Momma reflecting on her life all the while. Even when pain swelled in Big Momma's arthritic joints and her body rejected its stabs of insulin, she would sit in front of her picture window and bask in the sunshine, surrounded by the precious things she'd collected over her lifetime—porcelain prayer hands, brightly colored peacocks, a large black Bible, and miniature animal figurines—and dispensing her words of wisdom. "You catch more flies with honey," she would instruct. "Sometimes it's just good to listen, baby," and "Mark my words." But as she herself would also say, "Hearing a thang is much different from knowing and understanding a thang."

When I was five years old I began to follow as Big Momma re-traced the road our family had traveled. Then one hot day in June I was lost in a crowd and feared that I would be forever apart from my family. In that moment, I felt with a child's in-tensity the sadness I'd seen earlier in Big Momma's eyes as she recounted the ways in which black families had been pulled apart.

Big Momma had awakened me early that morning.

"Londa, do you have to pee?" she asked, wrestling me from my sleep.

"No, ma-a-am," I lied, and snuggled deeper under my quilt, made of old dresses and sewing scraps that still carried the faint aroma of mothballs.

With her hand on her hip and her tongue stuck in her bottom lip where there were no teeth to get in her way, Big Momma yelled in her singular language, "Onda, ge yo lying bu ou a ha bed befoe I burn yo af." *Londa, get your lying butt out of that bed before I burn your ass.* God forbid my bladder spill over. There were many things that Big Momma couldn't stand. Liars, lopsided cakes, and nosey neighbors sent her into a tizzy, but more than anything, Big Momma hated "pissy" sheets.

"And before you come in this kitchen, be sure to wipe dem hot spots," she said, to ensure that I wiped over my face, under-neath my arms, and between my legs. By this time the sound of bacon strips popping and the smell of buttered hoecakes filled me with anticipation.

After my sponge bath, I joined Big Momma, who was busy

reading the *Shreveport Sun,* the city's black newspaper, which contained every bit of news interesting to black folks. "Come give Big Momma a morning kiss," she coaxed. I obliged, but Big Momma did most of the kissing. "Is that enough bacon for you, baby?"

"Yes, ma'am," I said before bowing my head at the table. "Dear Lord, thank you for this day, this food, and Big Momma. Amen."

Big Momma went back to her paper, commenting to herself as I sat drinking buttermilk and catching grits and melting butter before it dripped off my plate. "Em, em. Bettie Jean done passed. Lord have mercy. I didn't even know she was sick. And it looks like dem lying, evil gray folks at the grocer are gon' have to hire some coloreds." Then, looking at me, she added, "It says here that Reverend Jones is gon' preach at the Juneteenth tent revival today."

"What's Juneteenth?" I asked.

"Juneteenth," Big Momma explained as she wiped my mouth, "is for us what the Fourth of July is to white folks. While I was still ironing for a living, we worked on the Fourth of July while the whites let us off for the nineteenth of June."

"So do I get to pop firecrackers?" I asked, hopeful.

"It's not about firecrackers, baby," Big Momma said, almost singing. "It's about being free."

"Yes, ma'am," I said, shrugging my shoulders.

"I told you how the white folks use to do us. Selling off people's kinfolks, whipping 'em, making them work in blistering fields and in their kitchens. They knew we was free two years before anybody told us."

"How'd we finally find out we were free?"

"We had to wait for that General Granger to get to Galveston,

Texas. That's where they announced it and word spread like a summer heat wave through Louisiana and Arkansas. Like everything else, nobody ever offered no explanation for why it took him two and a half years to get to us when he should have been there in a few months. Lord bless 'em, but that's how they do us." She shook her head.

"Were the slaves mad, Big Momma? Did they start fighting and burning up stuff?"

"Baby, no, they were happy. They just hollered and cried."

"But Big Momma," I asked, "everybody just went back to working the fields and cooking the meals, so what was the big deal about being free?"

"Cuz, baby, nobody could take you away from your family. You feel lost, like nothing, without your people. Don't you know, I'd kill somebody trying to take you from me, and Miss Hattie next door would be right there helping me."

"Oh," was all I said, but I wondered for a moment why anyone would want to take me from my family.

"Why you looking like that?" Big Momma asked. I still didn't understand this Juneteenth, so I asked Big Momma what went on there.

"You get to ride the Ferris wheel and carousel and eat all the pig's feet and barbecue ribs your belly can hold," Big Momma assured me, smiling.

I smiled back, hoping I'd be able to drink strawberry Shastas until my teeth turned colors.

"Reverend Jones has that big church across town," Big Momma said, mostly to herself. "I really got to dress up today."

"Can I wear one of my new halters?"

"I guess, but I don't know why yo' momma bought you something that lets your back hang all out."

After breakfast we cleaned up a bit and removed flapping sheets from the clothing line outside. Then we prepared for our big day. While I lotioned my legs and decided between red or blue shorts, Big Momma opened the door to her armoire, letting out a gush of pine scent that tickled my nose. She held a beige dress up to the light in one hand and a pale pink skirt and top in the other. I pulled my halter top out of its Sears wrapper and placed it on the bed next to my matching red shorts. Big Momma ultimately decided on a powder blue dress with flowers and pleats at the bottom. After pressing and repressing it, inspecting every corner for wrinkles, stains, or stray threads, she hung the cotton dress from the door frame, satisfied with its perfection. In the bathroom, she peered closely in the mirror as if staring through the pores of her angular face, then smoothed on Secret cream deodorant, curled her blue-rinsed hair, and inserted her teeth—"chop, chop."

After rolling up her stockings and snapping them to her girdle, Big Momma stepped into her dress. From a box that opened to the smell of perfume and the sound of a xylophone playing "Happy Birthday," she removed clip-on pearl earrings the size of nickels, a necklace of clear marble balls, and a matching bracelet.

After we'd dressed, Big Momma inspected everything—the kitchen stove, the bathroom faucet, our hair, and our clothes—one last time before ushering me outside. As she turned to lock the front door, I asked, "Why you always carry that umbrella, Big Momma?"

"Do you want me to pass out in this sun, girl? It's a hundred degrees out here."

"Nobody else uses an umbrella," I pointed out.

"Cuz they foolish. Now let's wend." After locking the front

door, Big Momma lifted the umbrella and kicked out her powder blue pumps. We became wayfarers, following the sunshine to another celebration.

The Juneteenth affair was held at Hamel's Park, a farm and carnival of games and rides. Intermingled were go-carts and cows, carousels and peacocks, life-size choo-choo trains, and one very large elephant. We were hardly in the park's gate before Big Momma's old friends embraced us with their long hugs and longer, cooing vowels. They fussed over me like I was a new pet. "Is this one of your babies? Come here and let me hug youuuuu," they said to me. I complied and was smothered in talcum powder and pillowy snuggles, then soothed with a few loose pieces of change.

We agreed that I could mind myself, but Big Momma still told the older kids from church to watch me. In case I needed something, she showed me where the church tent was. I could find her there.

"Here, baby," she said, leaving me with a needlepoint handkerchief tied tightly around four quarters, five dimes, and ten nickels. I spent the next few hours gobbling down cotton candy, barbecue ribs, and funnel cakes, making myself dizzy on the carousel, and fighting back the scorching sun with Shastas.

Around the time the fraternity step show ended, I felt the first throbs of a heat headache. Searching out Big Momma, I went inside a large tent, but instead of finding her among a church delegation, I observed men and women with a few straps of cloth around their privates standing onstage as though they were slaves up for auction. Just as the final bid for a sturdy woman went up, her children came running from backstage, crying and screaming, "Momma, don't go! Don't leave us!" Their momma turned her back to them, then collapsed right on top of her new master. Watching it, I grew sad and longed for my Big Momma even more.

In another tent I was nearly driven down by flashing red, silver, and blue go-carts racing along to fast music. I ran outside in a disheveled panic, and Big Momma's old friends found me there. "Ain't that Agnes's baby?" one said before rushing over to me.

"You all right, baby?" they asked. "Come on with us. We'll take you back to your Big Momma."

The church service was still going strong. The Masons and Eastern Stars sat like African royalty at the front of the tent nodding agreement with the preacher.

"Kings and queens we were before we were torn away from our families, and so we are again," the Reverend Jones said, pointing at the Eastern Stars wearing long white dresses with purple-and-gold, sashes draped across their chests and small thimble-shaped hats on their heads.

The old ladies walked me over to Big Momma, who was sitting at the edge of the crowd. Relieved, I climbed into her lap.

"I got lost, Big Momma. I'm so glad I found you," I said, squeezing her neck.

Big Momma kissed me hard on the forehead. "Rest, baby."

"Is the baby sick?" the lady next to Big Momma asked.

"She just had a little too much food and excitement. Drink this, Londa." I took a swig of the Pepto-Bismol that Big Momma removed from her purse and leaned my head into her neck and drifted off to sleep. My dreams, their images plucked from words my great-grandmother had shared with me—*mark my words . . . it's about being free . . . you feel lost without your people,* mixed with the words of the Juneteenth sermon that circled me—*the underground railroad . . . coded messages in*

spiritual songs . . . mothers holding their babies . . . slaves escap-
ing in the dark of night with only the light of burning wood to
guide them to the riverbank where freedom rested on the other
side. I looked across that river and saw majestic old ladies, the
tent coming out of the fog, and Big Momma standing in the
water to lead me to the safe places.

Momma Makes It Up the Hill

Lift up now thine eyes, and look from the place where thou art.

—Genesis 12:14

Momma and I were standing at one of the city's lowest corners watching the street flood while waiting for the bus to take us downtown. I was six, and she was twenty-five. The men eyed Momma in her patchwork boots and matching leather jacket, their mouths agape as if hoping to taste this nugget of dark chocolate.

It was cold and raining, and I was bundled under two sweaters and a clear plastic coat with seashells and water creatures painted all over it. As I twirled my matching umbrella, Momma looked at me and saw my face was turning ashy and dry. My mother despised ash, eye crud, and anything out of place, and she was quick to remove it. Unfortunately for me, that day she was out of lotion, so she spit in her hands and rubbed the moisture into my skin. Satisfied, Momma turned her attention to other concerns. She checked her watch, worried that for the first time since she'd had a job she would be late for work. Then, turning back to my frowning face, she announced, "We need a car."

"What are we gonna do with it, Momma?" I complained. "You can't drive."

"Don't you worry, Miss Sassy," she said, pulling my ponytail. "I'll figure it out."

Momma and I hadn't always taken the bus. Until I was four, my father, Jack (I couldn't remember ever calling him anything else), took us everywhere we needed to go, but he made us keep the windows rolled up tight. Better for us to smother than have anyone hear him yelling at Momma. In summer my only relief came from the breeze of an invisible crack that I could feel only when my face was pressed against the window. Momma and I would sit motionless, like dying butterflies inside a glass case.

That's just how my father thought of Momma—his beautiful specimen, which only he could handle or look at. He told her when she could speak, and slapped her if he thought she was returning another man's smile. He told her when it was time to go to bed, what to cook for dinner, and how long to stay in the bathroom. And he would never let her drive.

Momma had grown up the spirited sister of seven brothers. No one could have predicted such a fate for her. Her birth name was Gloria, though only her teachers called her that. To everyone else she was known as Kitty. Despite growing up the only girl in a houseful of raucous boys, Kitty had no tomboy qualities. She was as gentle a lady as her nickname suggested. By the time she was in high school, she would never leave the house without wearing a neatly pressed dress, high heels, and lipstick. Her beauty rested on her delicate features—smooth, spot-less, dark brown skin, a small poodle nose, and perfect white teeth. A walk down East Dalzell Street drew awkward one-liners from boys her age and long looks from the older men. "Ain't you a pretty black thang," they'd say. Momma, an honor-roll student and member of the Homecoming Court, paid them no mind. She was busy making plans for college up to the day my father called looking for someone else.

"You have the wrong number," Momma politely told him.

"You sound pretty," he replied. "What's your name?"

And life for Momma changed from there. It was the spring of her junior year, and she had only recently been allowed to take company in the front room. Jack, with his boxed cakes and daisies, made a good first impression. Momma was careful not to say anything that would raise their suspicions, but from the beginning, her relationship with Jack had been passionate and volatile. At six feet five, his thin frame towered over Momma's small body, and his brown eyes always held a misty sadness. Momma ignored the premature gray hair that streaked the left side of his head, warning of experiences beyond his nineteen years. She loved the unexpected flowers, the way he smiled when he looked at her, and how he seemed to need someone to love him.

My father was from the rough streets that drew a threatening line between Shreveport's downtown and a neighborhood called Allendale. Surrounding the few churchgoing folks there were hustlers, crapshooters, and drunks cluttering doorways. Momma, having never been allowed outside her front gate without one of her seven brothers, was naïve and didn't know how to navigate their courtship, which moved from the living room to Momma's school dances (Jack had dropped out a year earlier) and drive-in movies. Momma got pregnant, and as it would seem to any good Southern Baptist family, marriage was the only option. The wedding was planned and executed with excitement and urgency. Because the family was used to dreams being choked off, Momma's pregnancy and dashed state-college dream were not major disappointments. Besides, Jack had a good job at a manufacturing plant, and Momma was happy to make do at the community college. The newlyweds moved into a shotgun house even smaller than the one she grew up in. Each door led straight into another dark room. Momma and my father started their life together with pretty, cheap furniture and his ugly old problems. Both wore down quickly.

Secretly, Momma had grown accustomed to Jack's harsh words and hoped that the marriage could work. But then he started to hit her. After the first time, he said it would never happen again. It happened the next time he got drunk, then the time after that. Before long, Jack was beating Momma for breakfast, lunch, and dinner.

Momma spent the next four years of her marriage running from Jack. Sundays and holidays were the worst. One Christmas he bought Momma a beautiful pair of thigh-high suede boots. When she put them on and sashayed up and down the street in delight, he turned ugly and said she swayed her butt a little too much in the afternoon breeze. He worked himself into a rage and spent the better part of the evening beating her up the road in front of our house. Momma never knew what would make him turn cruel, so we lived with uncertainty, tension, and fear. Sometimes Momma and I would beat a hasty retreat out the front door. Once Jack cut us off and the bathroom had to serve as a temporary refuge. We formed a barricade with our backs against the door and prayed his drumming fists wouldn't break the hollow wood.

"Stop it," Momma had screamed. Unsure of whether her command was directed at my father's beatings or my nervous tic, I sat on my hands to keep from rubbing them together. Most times we were saved by a neighbor calling the police, imploring, "Y'all better come get that girl before that fool kills her." Members of the family, usually my grandparents, would try to persuade her to leave Jack and come back home, but she didn't want to take food from a table where it was already gravy thin, or bring two more bodies into a small house jammed with ten others, so she stayed.

Her relationship with Jack was nothing like what she'd seen in her parents' house, where Pappy's voice grew loud only when he laughed. And the only things she knew about romance had come from what she'd read in Harlequin novels, so naturally, she expected a happy ending.

But like a spring of water that gives and gives until without very much warning a rush turns to a trickle and then dries up, Momma gave and gave until she gave up. When she realized change wasn't coming, she made one herself.

On the mornings when she woke with fresh bruises on her face and throat, I'd watch Momma pack them down with ice before applying concealer under her eyes and on her cheeks. When her neck revealed strangulation, she'd wrap a brightly colored scarf delicately around the bruise. Later, she'd sit patiently in the car while my father drove her to Southern University's Shreveport commuter campus. Jack thought she was taking college classes there, but Momma had actually gotten a job as an operator at South Central Bell. As soon as his car would pull around the corner, Momma would run to catch the next bus headed downtown and toward her future—her own paycheck and freedom. Jack came home from work one day to find the police waiting for him to collect his things and be escorted from the property. But he didn't stay gone for long.

He came back late one night in early spring when I was four. The bedroom windows were open to draw out the heat of the day, and only the buzz of insects and the glow of streetlights filtered in as I slept with Momma. The repeated bangs on the front door woke us up. Momma had known enough to get the locks changed.

"That fool," she whispered, feeling blindly for the door. I sat up to go with her like I always did.

"Stay here," she told me, her gown flowing ghostlike in the breeze, so I stayed and listened wide-eyed. She opened the front door. She shouldn't have.

I heard my father's voice, slurred by Crown Royal.

"I need to come in. I left some money here."

"You didn't leave any money here," Momma replied defiantly. "Now go away."

"Let me see Londa."

"She's sleeping."

"I can see my baby sleep," he snarled, trying to push through.

"Not while you're drunk," Momma said, and stood back to close the door. Only the locked screen stood between them. It was enough to save her from the touch of Jack's angry hands but not from what he held in them.

I only dimly remember the sharp cracks of my father's gun— loud and painful, but gone in the time it takes to suck in a breath, or, in my Momma's case, to let out a scream as she stumbled to the floor. I don't remember how much time passed between my hearing Momma's first bloody gasp and sirens outside the front door. But suddenly the house exploded with frantic activity. The police arrived, too late to find my father, but the paramedics did keep Momma from bleeding to death. What I do remember is crouching on the floor in my pajamas tracing circles in a puddle of blood until my grandmother lifted me into her arms.

The next day I watched Momma lie in her hospital bed with little sponges plugging the holes that the bullets had dug into her body. One under her chin was about a quarter's breadth away from a rich vein in her neck. There were holes in her wrist, arm, shoulder, and chest. The doctors didn't want to remove the bullet over her heart. They said in time it would rise to the surface.

She couldn't hold me, but I stood in a chair and leaned over to look into her face, where she comforted me all the same.

"Momma, are you going to die?" I asked.

"No, baby," she said, lifting her unharmed arm slightly to tug on my hair.

"Are we going back to our house?"

"No, baby."

"Where we gon' live?" I wondered.

"We'll figure something out. Let's make like Eskimos," she said, and I rubbed my nose against hers.

Momma had only flesh wounds, so like her spirit, they quickly healed. Instead of letting my father's rage rise in her with bitterness and fear, Momma packed up those old memories like last summer's straw hats. The police eventually found my father and arrested him, but Momma declined to press charges as long as he left her alone. Against all probability and past experience, he did. And finally we started a new life. Momma went back to her job and began to save money, and bought us our very own home. It was a little brick house. The only thing grand about the place was the enormous hill on which it rested.

The year passed, with Momma getting a raise and my starting first grade at five years old. Then came another year and Momma said she was ready for another challenge. She got her driver's license and bought her first car—a white 1963 Chevrolet Impala that glistened like Momma's smile. It had a marbled, navy blue interior. We didn't care that our car was over ten years old. Like Momma, it had style, but in a way it was too bad that Momma had to drive it. She'd already deprived our Impala of its hubcaps. They'd popped off one by one during Momma's struggles with sidewalks and sharp corners. Whenever an eighteen-wheeler passed us on the highway, she closed her eyes tight. "Eeeee," she would shriek. I'd just shake my head from the backseat.

Momma got better at driving, and before long we were cruising the roads with almost no problems. She was signaling, making left turns, and keeping her eyes open on the highway. But the hill our house was on loomed over us like a mountain we'd never be able to climb. Her last hurdle was making it up our long, steep driveway without running over the hedges or scraping the house.

Every day there was a new attempt. She'd try entering from the left side of the street, then from the right. Sometimes we made a fast approach, other times we'd slow to a crawl, Momma huffing and puffing as if she was pushing the car instead of driving it and muttering, "Okay, okay. Today is the day." The result was always the same.

"Momma," I'd squeal, "you're on the grass already. You're never gonna make it up."

"Shut up, Yolanda," she'd yell, her head falling back on the headrest, her eyes resting on the ceiling. One day our neighbor Mr. Tanner stepped off his porch from where he'd been watching and began directing Momma up the hill. Mr. Tanner was at least eighty and bowlegged to the point of being crippled. He saw out of only one eye, but he was still a better driver than Momma.

"Turn it to the left, Kitty. No, no, not that far, girl. Bring it back toward the right. Now give her some gas." Every day it was the same thing. Momma would start up the hill with screeching tires only to end up in the hedges. Mr. Tanner knew what time to expect us and would wait in the middle of our large yard—a turtle atop a sandcastle. Over the weeks Momma became more proficient but still managed to scratch up the side of the car often enough. Eventually Mr. Tanner decided to stay in his front-porch swing and direct her with his hands.

One day, after a particularly precarious journey to the top that left chunks of our once-fat hedges caught in the right front tire, Mr. Tanner came over to the car. Momma sat embarrassed in the front seat, and I knew to stay quiet in the back.

"Now, Kitty," he said, "I been watching you drive up this hill every day the same way for the last two weeks. Why you so sure you can't do this?" Momma just stared ahead. "It's all in your head, Kitty. I want you to back this car up, go around the block, and get your mind fixed on getting up this hill."

Momma let out a sigh of exhaustion and wiped the mounting sweat from her face. Mr. Tanner tapped his cane on the hood of the car. "Look at me, girl," he said sternly. "Now, instead of hitting the hill like you're flying from the devil himself, you just slow down and drive this car up in your own sweet time. Once you turn in, straighten the car out, then give her a little more gas. All right?" he asked with a jack-o'-lantern smile. "Now go do it."

Mr. Tanner stepped back and waved his cane as we descended the hill. Momma rounded the block slowly, repeating the word "okay" over and over to herself. When we reached our driveway, she gazed up the hill. Momma did exactly what Mr. Tanner said. She slowed down and turned the car into the driveway. When it was straight, she applied a bit more gas, and in a measured pace we ascended our cement mound. She looked not to the left or to the right but directly ahead. I peered out the back window and watched as we continued to climb.

"You're doing it, Momma!" I called out. Momma smiled, nodded, and kept on going.

When the Impala made it to the summit, Mr. Tanner smiled from his porch swing and tipped his hat. Momma and I sat in the car for a minute savoring her victory and listening to the engine push out its last breath before winding down. I leaned my head out the window to see if Momma had snagged even an inch of grass—she had not. Momma grabbed hold of my ponytail and gently pulled my head back into the car, saying, "See, I told you I'd figure it out." I smiled at her and began to roll up my window. "No," she said, "keep it down. We're going for another ride." With that we slid back down the hill and roared off into the fading daylight. As the moon rose over us, we turned across the miles of dirt road and highway that lay ahead.

May Day

The waters piled up. The surging waters stood firm like a wall;
the deep waters congealed in the heart of the sea.... They sank
as lead in the mighty waters.

—*Exodus 15:8–10*

This morning was different. For starters, I was awakened by the ranting of a wood warbler outside my window. Since I clung desperately to every last drop of sleep, normally this would have annoyed me. But I noticed hanging in my closet the blue shorts and matching top Honeymoon had sewn for me using bandanna scarves. *Today is May Day,* I thought, smiling to myself. Then Momma appeared.

All she said was "Rise." But I caught something in her voice.

She progressed swiftly, removing from my top drawer a pair of yellow panties with the word SATURDAY inscribed on the front. My shoe box of a suitcase was open on the bed, and already stacked inside were a white slip, new socks, and a dress nicer than the ones I usually wore over the weekend.

"Momma, am I going somewhere?" I asked.

"Yes," she said, turning to deposit my toothbrush, children's Bible, and collapsible umbrella into the side panel.

"Is it going to storm?"

"I don't know," Momma admitted, "but if there is a downpour, you'll be prepared." Then she kneeled and cupped my cheeks in her hands, hoping they would still the news. "Yolanda, you're spending the night with your father."

The beat of my heart lapsed, along with my speech. In my confusion, I struggled to understand why Jack would appear on this day. May Day, I knew from my teachers, was a celebration of the working class. These were people like my family and neighbors who sweated their lives away inside factories to feed their families. Jack wasn't a part of that. He couldn't keep a job and didn't know how to treat his family.

"What does he care about May Day?" I demanded to know, my tears streaming down Momma's hands.

"Oh, baby, he's not coming because it's May Day. He's coming because he's your father." It was the sort of pat answer a parent could offer a child. Only Momma believed it was enough. I hadn't seen Jack in over two years. Not since the night he'd tried to kill Momma and then hidden cowardly under a neighbor's porch. I spent the entire morning worrying over what it would be like to have Jack back.

Later at school my classmates and I formed circles around a tree-high pole with colorful strips of fabric cascading from its top. To keep my ribbon from thrashing in the wind, a knot as tight as the muscles in my stomach secured the piece to a stake. After freeing the knot, I held my end while my eyes followed with the blue ribbon up to where the sun was fighting the clouds. As I began to wrap the cloth around the pole, I shouted with the others, "May Day, May Day." The strong winds tugged at the ribbon, but I refused to surrender it. When we were finished twisting the strips and scraps together, I stood back to see that the timber's splintered imperfections had been covered over and now the pole looked like a cordon of red, white, and blue silk. Pleased with the transformation, I smiled and, for a little while, enjoyed myself. But in the late afternoon, the clouds broke open and my joy washed away with the rain. As I made my way down the street, I knew that a visit from Jack awaited me, and my stomach dipped like a rowboat caught in a monsoon. By the time I had completed my daily walk up the rickety steps leading to Honeymoon's porch, my white sneakers, soaked to beige, were making squishy sounds. I peered through the screen and saw my grandmother cleaning the stovetop.

"Londa, is that you?" she called out, my name rolling like water off her tongue.

"Yes, ma'am," I answered, tossing my wet shoes in the corner.

"Come on in here and get something to eat before you have to go with your lying daddy," she beckoned. Leaving her Brillo pad for a moment, she pulled down a bowl for me and spooned it full of warm cinnamon bread pudding.

Instead of devouring the pudding as I usually did, I picked out the raisins and watched Honeymoon empty out old cooking grease and scrub away the burn scars on her coffee percolator. The stove eyes that she'd covered in aluminum foil stared up at me, reflecting tiny bolts of light off the walls.

"You not hungry this afternoon?" Honeymoon asked, looking down at me. I shrugged.

"You just nervous about going with that sorry daddy of yours. I don't blame you, though."

I searched Honeymoon's face. It was perfectly round, like a full moon. That's how she got her nickname—for that, and for being sweet as honey. She was actually more like a stem of ripe sugarcane, with that sweet layer buried underneath a toughness. She took in every stray dog and man who showed up at her door, but her fury fell on those who harmed her children. It was no wonder she spit every time she heard Jack's name.

"I told your momma ain't no reason you should have to go anywhere with that no-good man." I gave a little nod, encouraging her to continue. "Your poor momma just struggles to take care of you, and she can't even count on that sorry something to send her fifty dollars a month. But watch how important he's gon' act when he comes in here today."

Honeymoon's resentment toward my father festered long after Momma's wounds had healed. Momma could hardly remember what had happened the night Jack shot her, but Honeymoon couldn't make herself forget. The neighbors, having heard gunshots, called Honeymoon before phoning the police. My grandmother didn't even manage to change out of her old bleach-stained nightgown. She just grabbed her robe, the quilted one with the stuffing hanging from its side, and hurried down the street to Momma's house. She stood over Momma's bloodied body, collecting herself by tightening her robe's worn sash and reassuring me that Momma was going to be all right.

Even though Honeymoon's Bible told her it was right to forgive, she couldn't bring herself to release Jack. My feelings couldn't be explained so simply. Even a memory as thin and benign as my father making me runny grits on a Sunday morning was tangled with my broader recollection of the curses, mean looks, and licks he'd showered on Momma. Resentment, pity, and attachment—it was an exacting task trying to untangle my emotions.

"I don't see why I have to go," I said, watching as Honeymoon's eyes grew wide.

"You don't, Londa," she whispered conspiratorially. "This is what we gon' do. When he comes, you look real sad. Once he says it's time for you to go, you fall out screaming. Just cut the fool. When he reaches for you, act like you having convulsions and run to the back of the house."

Jack and his aunt Patty came late that afternoon. He carried flowers for Honeymoon, a box for me. He smiled through the currents of tension, acting as if very little time had passed since he'd been inside that door.

"Open your present," he said to me. I lifted the white lid, dropped the box, and screamed at the sight of a white rabbit jacket that appeared to breathe. The gift revealed how little my father knew about me.

"What's wrong?" he asked, seemingly bewildered, but really just pressing me to be appreciative.

"I don't like fur," I said, feeling a sob bubble up in my throat.

"Why? Daddy spent a lot of money for this."

"Jack, what you mean by that?" Honeymoon countered, eager to attack. "I don't care how much you spent. You better get that thang away from Londa. She don't like rabbits, and she's terrified of fur."

Sensing frustration swell up in Jack, Aunt Patty, whose only job, it seemed, was to placate everybody, patted him soothingly on the back. "Don't worry about it, Jack. Let's just get Yolanda and go."

In that moment I wanted to kick Aunt Patty square in her butt. I'd always liked her, but she made me mad right then. She was taking Jack's side. If I hadn't been sure about enacting Honeymoon's scheme before, the coat called me to action. When Jack reached for me, I shrieked and viciously shook my head no. "I don't want to go!" I cried, moving toward my grandmother, "Honeymoon, don't make me go. Please, Lord. I don't want to go."

Jack was startled. Dew formed on his eyelids. "Yolanda, I'm your daddy. I won't hurt you," he promised. Two years had passed since I'd heard the gunshots, but I remembered. His voice and face never left me, thanks to sporadic phone calls and a picture he had sent of himself in his Army coat and hat. He'd been discharged from the military just as he had been from other jobs, but I had liked that the picture portrayed my father as handsome and responsible.

Honeymoon cut Jack off. "Well, boy, I can't let you take Londa behaving like this. You know, after she witnessed what you did to her momma, her stomach flipped and tossed for some time. I can't risk you messing up her system like that again." And she showed him to the door.

Momma was furious when she came home and found out what Honeymoon and I had done. She said we looked like skunks after a day of pissing on everybody. Honeymoon, busy dragging a straw broom across her thin carpet, barely gave Momma a second glance.

Momma, in her homemade red skirt and blouse, circled Honeymoon slowly, giving her the evil eye. "Yolanda's a child, and she goes where I tell her to go. And you, Mother, need to learn a little something about grace and forgiveness."

Honeymoon placed a hand on her cocked right hip. "Not with that good-for-nothing I don't."

"Mother," Momma said, stuffing her purse into an armchair to free up her finger for pointing, "don't you ever talk about Jack like that in front of Yolanda. Don't give her that spirit. He's her father, and we're always going to respect that."

Honeymoon let out a "humf" and went back to sweeping her carpet.

Then Momma turned her eyes down on me. "Why did you do that, Yolanda? Has Jack ever touched you?"

"No, ma'am," I said, ashamed, "but I don't want to go anywhere with him."

Momma placed the palm of her hand in the middle of my back and pulled me into her warm, soft self. "Don't you know that man loves you and you're all he's got?" she said. "I'm sorry Jack is what you're stuck with, but he is your daddy and there's nothing we can do about that. You've got to figure out a way to get along with him. Do you understand?"

"Do you like Jack, Momma?" I asked, locking my eyes on hers.

She looked down at her left wrist, where a snail-shaped scar remained. "Sometimes I think I've forgiven him. Most of the time I can't stand him, but I don't want that to have anything to do with you. You've got to get to know him for yourself."

Because Momma was always honest with me, I trusted her even when what she said didn't seem to make much sense. I was still troubled, feeling caught in the middle, with Honeymoon wanting me to go in one direction and Momma turning me in another. I felt like I did when we were wrapping the Maypole with that stubborn wind teasing us—from one side pushed forward and from the other fighting not to be thrown back.

The next day Jack and Aunt Patty came back, everyone having agreed on a compromise. I would go with them to lunch.

"You ready?" His words came quickly, at once a statement and a question. Jack arched his body forward as if he were going to tip his cowboy hat to me, but instead he dropped his pleading eyes down to the hems of his wide-legged gabardine pants. He probably hoped that his voice wouldn't stir in me a spell of histrionics the way it had the day before.

I peered at him through Honeymoon's screened door, a door not much different from the one he had shot Momma through. "There's always something between us," he said with a pained smile.

I felt sorry for him. I thought maybe I wanted to give him a big hug around his neck and a fat kiss on the cheek, but right then all I could muster was a tentative "Yeah" before stuffing my hands into my dress pockets.

"Be good, Londa. Love you," Honeymoon said before casting threatening eyes on my father.

I gave Honeymoon the hug and then took Jack's outstretched hand. Aunt Patty sat in the back, not quite invisible. As Jack drove toward the highway I looked back, expecting to see Honeymoon standing on her porch, but instead my eyes gazed beyond her house to my school playground, where the usually ugly, discolored poles now flaunted magnificent colors.

"Those are for you," Jack said, pointing to the floor and a large mason jar full of quarters.

"Wow," I said, using both hands to lift the jar from the floor. "How many are in here?"

"I don't know, but I'll bet it makes you the richest girl in first grade. Every time I would put one in there, I'd think of Daddy's little girl. How do you like the sound of that?" Jack pressed. I acted as if I hadn't heard him, pretending instead to be enthralled by the jar of quarters. A dumb smile froze on his face.

The quarters had come from Jack's tips—for luggage toting, cab driving, and coat hanging. Jack always got big tips because he was good at first impressions—the sad smile, the small, unthreatening hands, the unassuming compliments all worked to his advantage, so quarters had undoubtedly been easy to come by. Maintaining that first impression was another story. Something always happened, something that was always someone else's fault.

I didn't know what to say to him, so I started counting the quarters I'd poured into the lap of my skirt. This was Jack's way of trying to win me over with a grand gesture. He didn't understand that to build a lasting relationship, he had to start with the kind of little things that Momma provided, like my hand-painted yellow chair and the snack that awaited me every day after school. I loved Momma so much because I knew those little things took a lot of effort. She didn't mind doing them because she knew they made me feel special.

When I thought it was safe, I looked over at Jack. The never-changing smile was still there. It was the one he wore when complimenting the ladies on their dresses or brushing lint off a gentleman's jacket. It was also the one he wore moments before slapping Momma across the face. The smile was like the lyrics to a song that didn't take on meaning until its music gave it context. Watching him, I noticed his eyes were shaped like mine and wondered if his gray signs of worry would also show up in my hair. Momma sometimes reminded me that I also had his temper.

"Where we going?" I asked.

"Where do you want to go?"

"Freeman & Harris."

"That old beat-up place? I was thinking of someplace classy like Ralph and Kacoos."

I stared off thinking for a moment, then said, "Spell *Kacoo's*."

"K-A-C-O-O-'S, I think. Your daddy's not that great a speller." But he was right this time.

"Did someone take you there?" he asked, disappointed.

"No, but I don't want to go there." Momma and I had passed the restaurant many times. With the wind whipping my face, I would sound out the name of Ralph and Kacoo's along with the words on other billboards, church doors, business mastheads, and street signs. It was one of the ways Momma had taught me to read. I'd often seen old white ladies with butterfly combs adorning their beehives drive up to the restaurant's front door and hand the keys to their polished pastel Cadillacs to the young men who stood out front. Momma said we'd go there one day, but it had to be a special occasion.

"You'll like it," Jack assured me. Being around people like that made Jack's sail stand up.

"No, I won't. You said we could go wherever I wanted," I charged, feeling my neck stiffen until I was sure it would snap.

"Jack," Aunt Patty offered feebly from the backseat. "Take her where she wants to go."

Like a spurned child, he relented. "Okay. We can go where you want. You don't have to get upset."

"I want to go home."

"No, you can't go home," he said. Having no other choice, I kicked my legs out and sent quarters crashing into the windshield and plunging to the floor.

"Yolanda, pick up those quarters," he yelled.

"Don't you scream at me," I shouted back. "What are you going to do next? Hit me?" I braced myself for a showdown.

"Is everything all right up there?" Aunt Patty intervened to keep the peace, but not before Jack's face shattered into a hundred pieces.

"Yolanda," he said softly, "I'd never hit you." It was true. Jack had never hit me. I seemed to be the only thing he loved to the point of self-control.

"Yolanda, are you all right, sweetheart?" Aunt Patty asked, leaning up to rub my hair. My heart sank, and I wished, in that moment, that I could be friends with my daddy. I started by picking up the quarters.

Jack pulled up to Freeman & Harris, the windowless eating house that pouted from a downtown corner. In spite of its grubby look, all Shreveport life passed through its doors. White businessmen dined alongside black preachers, families ate Sunday dinner, and high school couples enjoyed postprom meals of stuffed shrimp and lemonade. Even visiting dignitaries dined on meals served on cafeteria plates. Outside, small-town hookers and alley-cat gamblers lined the sidewalks. Those were the people that Jack knew. That was where he was from, the place he came back to. It was who he was, but he didn't want me to know it. Here he had to park his own car.

My eyes struggled to adjust inside the cavernous building. Table chatter and the sound of forks clinking mingled with the ten Motown songs that replayed on the jukebox. A waiter wearing an orthopedic shoe limped toward us, smiling. "Whatcha gon' have, pretty little girl?" he asked, blowing me a kiss. Jack immediately snapped.

"You talking to my daughter like that?" he shouted in the waiter's direction.

"I'm sorry, Jack. We grew up together. Brother, you know I didn't mean no harm. Don't you remember me?"

"Sure he does," Aunt Patty chimed in, looking encouragingly at Jack. "He lived over behind us."

But Jack didn't want me to know that he was familiar with the cripple, so he said, "Man, I don't know you."

The man walked away quickly, and like old times, Jack turned his rage on Momma.

"Your Momma brings you here? I thought she had class, but she don't." As soon as the words left his mouth, I felt my body sink into the chair, but I didn't want him to know he was taking me under.

"My momma's got class and brains and everything you ain't got," I said, snaking my neck.

"What that's suppose to mean?" he asked, but I could tell he didn't want to know.

"When's the last time you paid child support? You know I don't just eat when you come to town every two years."

"See. That's the kind of thing your momma says to you about me."

"She don't say nothing bad about you, man, but if I want to go to McDonald's and she doesn't have any money, and I say, did my 'daddy' send me any, what's she suppose to do? Lie for your sorry self?"

"Well, I'm here feeding you now, so what do you want?"

"Everybody just needs to calm down," Aunt Patty butted in.

I looked at Jack as hard as I could and said I wouldn't take a peanut out of his hand if we were the last people on the face of the earth. There was more I wanted to say too. I wanted to say that Momma was a good woman and he had been a fool to treat her the way he had, to tell him that his arrogance, his ignorance, and his violent temper had forced us to move on without him, but I couldn't find the words. I began to cry.

Jack leaned down to rub my face and I saw my eyes again and heard Momma's voice saying, "You look just like your daddy."

"You two gotta learn to talk nice to each other," Aunt Patty urged. "Y'all need each other. Now kiss and make up."

I couldn't muster a kiss, but I did want to do something. The only thing I could think of was to recount for them the May Day celebration we'd had at school the day before. I told Jack about how the woven scraps had worked like a quilt, coming together to form something beautiful.

"I wish I'd been there," he said, grateful for the reprieve. I smiled and said it would be on the same day next year.

On the drive back to Honeymoon's, sheets of rain seemed to lift the car underneath us. As we passed my school, I looked to point out the Maypole to them, but it had fallen over in the rain. Its colors were swathed in mud. When we reached Honeymoon's house, Aunt Patty kissed me for reassurance and whispered a plea in my ear: "Give your daddy a hug."

Jack and I walked slowly up to Honeymoon's front door. Before I went inside, he bent down to face me with my own eyes again.

"Can I have a hug and hear you call me Daddy before I leave?" With the wind at my back, I placed my hands around his neck.

"Bye, Daddy," and as soon as I said it my stomach loosened its grip on me. Perhaps I was learning a little something about grace and how it could cover Jack's imperfections as well as my own.

Baptism or Brimstone

> If you will be kind to these people and please them and give them
> a favorable answer, they will always be your servants.
>
> —*II Chronicles 10:7*

My grandfather, Pappy, always said there was one of two ways to do a thing: wholeheartedly or half-baked, the right way or the wrong, by baptism or by brimstone. If we were rough and forceful with the thing we craved, Pappy said, it would fall away from us, like petals on a flower touched by a careless hand. You could tell the method Pappy preferred by the way he tended his yards and treated his family. After work, he'd burst into the kitchen covered in dirt from a day of spreading bonemeal around flower beds, reviving neglected black walnut trees by pouring water and dressings over their roots, and trimming silky green grass down to an even inch and a half.

When the smell of gasoline and grass filtered through the house and made our noses itch we knew that Pappy was home. The family would stop whatever we were doing and gather around him.

"Hello, Missus," he would say to Honeymoon, and pass his calloused hands across her face and back. I never heard the word pass between them, but you could see the love there.

Pappy was from a backwoods Louisiana town called Stonewall. Its muddy streets were an improvement over the foot-plowed trails between the houses behind Main Street. His mother had died in childbirth, so he grew up on a farm under the care of his grandmother, brothers, and sisters. At eight, he left grade school and continued his tutelage in fields, where he learned to hunt, plow, and harvest. Hearing about the high pay and good life in the city, Pappy trotted up to Shreveport to find work.

He met his future wife on "Big Sunday" in a pasture of grazing cows where her church had gathered for a lakeside baptism of new believers. Honeymoon had gone over to the ice cream truck to buy a soda pop. On the passenger side of the white trolley, Pappy leaned forward and served the drink with a grin. They began courting, which according to my grandmother amounted to attending church service together on Sundays and sitting close to each other while watching the news or baseball on this new contraption called a TV.

By the time I came along, they had been married for almost two decades and had raised a houseful of children. Even the ones who had grown up and moved away couldn't stay gone. Momma and I were there so much, I sometimes called their house home, and the oldest boy, my uncle Rat, brought his family in from Arkansas most weekends. I came to associate one such visit with both baptism and brimstone.

Pappy had come in from an afternoon of Saturday yard work and instructed one of his younger boys to bring him his firewater—a cheap liquor called Ten High, a gift from one of his yard owners the Christmas prior. Pappy's middle boy,

Jackie, who was not yet seventeen, reached in the back of the china cabinet and poured Pappy a sip.

"What did you do today, old goat?" Jackie taunted his father playfully.

Pappy, delighted by the question, leaned back in his usual manner. "Well," he started, "I pruned back some oak trees that were threatening to fall down a hill. I planted some flowers that should bloom real nice this winter, and I got a good watering in. I mean I drenched that grass and the like with so much water I could hear the roots gulping it down. Most folks sprinkle just a little here and there," Pappy said, tilting his head as if pouring water from a cup. "But you got to drown 'em in water."

"What you say, Deacon?" Jackie said, waving a finger in the air like a preacher. "You gotta baptize them plants and trees in the name of the Father, the Son, and the Holy Ghost."

"That's right, that's right," Pappy said, the kitchen raining mirth. Pappy was always real easy with us. He'd left the bossing to Honeymoon, and when she was away cleaning houses, Uncle Rat carried out his overseer duties with regularity and seriousness. But their oldest was always mindful to distribute the food evenly, complete the chores, and protect his siblings from neighborhood bullies.

Uncle Rat called all the shots with an even temper—until the day he met Aunt Shirley. She caused his heart to erupt, his body to quiver. He was still a teenager working at the city hospital mopping up spills, scrubbing toilets, and moving things with tall ladders. That's where she first spotted him, up high, balancing a package with arms that seemed stuffed with stones. Deciding right then that she wanted him, Aunt Shirley gathered her short maid's skirt between her thighs, placed her left foot high up on the ladder, and beckoned him. He drew near, ignoring the stern warning from his mother's sister, Doll, who also worked at the hospital.

"Boy," his aunt cautioned him, "you know a black girl who looks like that goes through men like they were sunflower seeds—sucking 'em in, spitting 'em out. She already got one baby on her hip and seems hard-pressed to get another one soon. You leave her alone. She's trouble, you hear?"

But Uncle Rat only heard Aunt Shirley's husky voice as she looked at him through sugar-brown eyes and laid her body over his. When a job hauling pulpwood through the mountains of Arkansas came his way, Uncle Rat packed up Aunt Shirley and her baby boy and made a family of his own. Even though they came often, that Saturday we waited for them as if years had passed since their last visit.

Just as the sun faded into the trees, Honeymoon pulled a kitchen chair out to the porch where Pappy sat in a broken rocker with the boys. The tethering porch threatened me with creaking noises as I sprang from its ledge. Its edges, sagging from too much weight and not enough care, seemed to frown as if aware of the burden ahead.

Uncle Rat finally pulled up with Aunt Shirley and their new baby next to him in the cab of his green truck. Out of its bed leaped their other children—two short, man-faced little boys and their shy sister, Betty. I called her my twin cousin because we were both seven. Walking slowly behind them was Uncle Rat with his hand locked around his wife's denim-clad hips. Uncle Rat had everything in his life that Pappy did—a job that suited him, children of his own, and a wife whom he loved, only Aunt Shirley wasn't the cook, wife, or mother he'd expected her to be, making it difficult for him to assume Pappy's laid-back manner.

"Hey, boy," everybody said as the family approached the yard, even though Uncle Rat was a man with a neck the size of a fire log and muscles that poured down his arms like thick resin from a maple. His arrival and the sting of mosquitoes sent everybody back into the house. Honeymoon filled plates with collard greens, smothered turkey wings, and corn bread. After we had crammed ourselves full, the brothers busied themselves with setting up the stereo and card table. During spades there were no smiles, just malt liquor, cigarettes, and a stack of cards—the high ones being jokers, aces, and the two of spades, which Uncle Rat now held, trumping them all.

"Game, baby," he called out, slamming the cards down hard, causing the table to tremble, then kissing his wife dead on her full, pink lips. They celebrated their victory with a slow dance in the middle of Honeymoon's living room. Uncle Rat moved his hands down Aunt Shirley's back to her waist, then grabbed her butt. The small fleshy body rolled underneath Uncle Rat's hands like pie dough. His wife smiled as he mouthed the words to the song "You Sexy Thang" into her ear. They were still young—Aunt Shirley, the mother of four children, was barely twenty-five—and the way they looked at each other could ignite a room.

Watching them dance, Honeymoon shook her head disapprovingly and turned back to Betty, whom she was helping to remember the Ten Commandments.

"Thou shalt not kill," Betty recited. "Thou shalt not steal. Thou shalt not commit adultery. Thou shalt not . . . uhhh . . ."

"Have any engraven images," I blurted.

"Londa, nobody's talking to you," Honeymoon said. "Betty, baby, you're doing good. Now just start over." Betty was older than I was by about five months, but looking at us, you'd think

I had her by more than a year. While Betty was puny, I was tall, with a chunky butt. I had already grown in two large front teeth before Betty even lost her first set, and I had finished reading the Jack and Jill series while she was still trying to master the alphabet. She was always peeping from behind somebody with her five plaits in the shape of jumbo shrimp poking from her head. My loudness drowned out her quiet.

"Thou shalt not kill. Thou shalt not steal. Thou shalt not . . . Honeymoon, I can't remember," Betty said. Exasperated, she moved her thumb up to her mouth.

"Miss Betty," her mother called out, "what have I told you about sucking your thumb? You're a big girl. Big girls don't suck their thumbs."

"She's just a baby," Uncle Rat insisted, pulling Shirley closer.

Honeymoon interrupted their petting. "I want to know why y'all not teaching this baby her commandments?" Waving her finger in the air, she added, "The Bible says, 'Impress these commandments on your children.' Now that's what the Word says." The couple brushed Honeymoon off with a playful wave and moved outside to dance with the fireflies.

"Fire and brimstone for the two of you," Honeymoon said as the screen door closed.

"What's brimstone?" I asked, looking at Honeymoon.

"It's burning rock, so hot it glows. It's what the devil burns in hell. It's the hard way to go," Honeymoon guaranteed with a sour face.

Suddenly, we heard a board snap and a woman scream. Everyone rushed outside in unison, like water breaking through a dam. Aunt Shirley had slipped on a loose plank and fallen beneath the porch.

As we peered between the wooden boards at Aunt Shirley's

still body, a chill of worry crept up my back with the cool fall air. Together the boys pulled her up from the moist black dirt. Uncle Rat and Pappy laid her on Honeymoon's giant bed. Her pale skin, dotted with soil, looked like freshly picked cotton. Her new hair color, the yellow red of a pomegranate, was now smothered by leaves. Pappy waved under her nose the smelling salts he kept on hand to revive the women who passed out after shouting at church.

"Shirrrley," Honeymoon called out, dabbing the sleeping face that had turned puce. "If she don't come to, we'll have to call an ambulance."

After a few long seconds, Aunt Shirley coughed and opened her eyes.

"You all right, baby?" Uncle Rat asked, crawling into bed beside her to remove the dead leaves from her hair.

"All right," Honeymoon said. "Excitement's over. Everybody go to bed."

Uncle Rat lifted Aunt Shirley and carried her to the back bedroom. I was spending the night with Betty, so we lay down facing each other on the sofa outside her parents' room.

"I thought Momma was dead," Betty said, considering whether to suck her thumb even though Aunt Shirley would smack her good if she caught her doing it.

"Has your momma been baptized?" I wondered.

"I don't know. I think so." Betty's eyes drifted off between sleep and ponderance.

"You know you burn in hell if you die without being baptized," I said gravely, trying to keep her up with me. "You heard what Honeymoon said it's like down there—burning rock everywhere, glowing like coals just set on fire."

"Uhhh," Betty mumbled as her eyes fell on the wide crack in

her parents' bedroom door. Moans and the whispering of sheets had grabbed her attention. Curiosity outweighing our fear of being caught, we crawled across the dark floor and peeked in.

The sheets were off the bed, and Uncle Rat's body covered Aunt Shirley's. His darkness melted into her pink flesh like Neapolitan ice cream. He kissed her all over. His large body seemed suddenly soft, and I imagined heat rising from him. I could see how much he loved Aunt Shirley. It was apparent from the way his eyes drooped down and looked at her. It was in the tone of his voice when he called her name or just said, "baby." It was in his arms, in the way he held her. He was more than uncovered. Embarrassed, Betty and I tiptoed back to bed.

"Your daddy's sucking your momma's milk," I opined, having witnessed a neighbor breast-feeding a few weeks earlier. "You go to hell for that too, but they're married, so it's okay, I think."

"That's good," Betty said before falling asleep with her thumb in her mouth. I followed behind her with thoughts of love and fire in my head.

The next morning, Honeymoon got us up to attend Saint Peter Baptist, which was squeezed between a ditch and a highway. Walking inside its swinging double doors, what I always noticed—before the sloping floor, the wobbly pews, or the ushers' pilgrim shoes—was the feeling of the place, conveyed in a wink from my favorite deacon, the floral aroma of my Sunday-school teacher's perfume, and no less than a hundred familial greetings. Though the church provided little in the way of comforts, it possessed what was needed for salvation—Honeymoon assured us of that. Still, there was one thing we all loathed—the stifling heat unrelieved by the stingy air conditioner and creased Winfield Funeral Home paper fans, which worsened once folks packed the aisles during Pastor Green's lengthy homilies.

The subjects of these sermons ranged from creation to damnation to redemption. And I am fairly certain that this Sunday's message touched on one of those themes, but what truly got my attention and has stayed in my memory all these many years was his grand invitation to discipleship. Pastor Green stepped from the pulpit into the aisle and placed a chair there. Then our minister, small in stature and possessing a duck's features—a beak nose, small mouth, and big feet protruding from his robe like black flippers—flung his arms wide and said in a voice like thunder, "The doors of the church are open. Any man, woman, or child who has not accepted Jesus Christ as your Savior should come now and avoid the road to hell."

When no one came forward, the deacons and the choir urged, "Come on, Pastor ... there's someone here ... amen, amen."

Over the chorus, Pastor roared on. "You think these little problems we have right now are something. These small troubles in our homes, disruptions with our children, and frictions on our jobs are nothing. None of that compares to the fire and brimstone that the Word tells us is coming to nonbelievers. Now I want to keep you from that. All you have to do is confess Jesus Christ as your Savior and keep the Lord's commandments in your heart."

As the organist began to play "Amazing Grace" I turned to Betty, pretending to read her church program, and asked her, in a way she knew was not a question, to go up with me.

I understand that some people experience a dramatic unfolding the moment before they accept Christ. Years later, they can tell you the instant they were changed, born again. I had no such encounter that day. I got swept up in an emotional wave of heat, majestic organ music, and the fear of burning in hell. The night before, I'd wrestled with a horrible dream of leaping from the front porch into a pit of fire while Pappy sprayed me with his water hose and Honeymoon shouted out Scriptures to keep me from burning. Recalling all this while Pastor Green pleaded for a soul, I experienced what was more a panic than a calling, but in either case, I felt compelled to move. I motioned for Betty to walk with me. She followed me down the aisle.

As we neared him, Pastor reached for our hands. He kneeled before me and asked, "Do you have something you'd like to say to the church, Yolanda?"

A fainthearted "Yes" in a voice no louder than a whisper was all that was ever expected of the young, but I took the microphone, covered it with my mouth, and amplified, "I accept the Lord Jesus Christ as my Savior, and I want to be baptized."

Pastor then handed the microphone to Betty, who repeated what I had said. Momma sat proudly silent in the choir box next to Honeymoon, who kept shouting joyfully, "Hallelujah," while holding herself as though she was about to start her Holy Ghost dance. "A child shall lead them," came another chant from an elder as Betty and I knelt on weak knees in front of them.

Pastor snapped his black robe up like a hawk extending its wings and declared, "These two have accepted. For those among you who have not, I give you this final opportunity." When no one else came forward, he added somberly, "The blood of Christ is on your hands."

A great deal of fanfare surrounded our getting baptized and

two sets of clothes—a new white dress for the first Communion, an old ragged one suitable for water dunking, and a rubber swimming cap. Naturally, Betty's and my baptism required
a few weeks of planning, and this technicality proved calami-
tous for Betty, because when Uncle Rat heard about it, he said
he didn't care where the blood was, Betty was too young to get
baptized.

"Well, big brother," Momma had responded, "we disagree. If
my child is old enough to utter the name of the Lord and confess with her own mouth, she is old enough to get baptized."

"Well, that's you," Uncle Rat retorted, "but like I said, Betty
ain't getting baptized."

"It ought to be all right with you too," Momma said sharply.

"I tell you what, little sister. You be the man of your house,
and I'll be the man of mine. Betty is too young to join church.
She is just doing what she saw Yolanda do."

No one was sure if Uncle Rat really didn't want Betty to be
baptized or if he was just mad at Aunt Shirley, who'd left him in
bed early that morning with the claim that she too was going to
church, but no one saw her there. Hours later, she appeared
from a car on the corner, her lips carrying the tint of faded lipstick. Over dinner she heard of the day's occurrence and broke
with her husband. "Rat," she asked, "what does it hurt the girl
to get baptized even if she is a little young?"

"Shirley," Uncle Rat yelled, his neck tightening to reveal
large veins, "you know better than to question me right now.
Betty is not getting baptized."

"Rat, I don't have a problem with it," his wife said.

Uncle Rat just glared at her and said, "Later."

"Later" meant that around midnight, when the autumn
leaves glowed like fire under the streetlights, Uncle Rat would

take Aunt Shirley into the woods across the street and hit her. Pappy, hearing Aunt Shirley scream, would run across the street, his blood curdling, his bare feet kicking aside the yellow leaves. He would bring the woman bruised and crying back into the house. Betty and I would watch and listen as Pappy told Uncle Rat that he had not acted in the right way. Honeymoon would dab Aunt Shirley's sore spots with rubbing alcohol and whisper Bible verses into her ear. *Weeping endures for a night. Joy comes in the morning.* The talking, crying, and praying would go on all night.

"Son," I heard Pappy say, "you gon' rule your house. But are they gon' follow you admiringly like you's a morning star or with a quickening for fear of your wrath? You can only boss people for a season."

That was what Pappy meant by baptism or brimstone. Compassion and gentle-heartedness are the forces we need to pull others toward us. Jealousy and fear, even if they work for a little while, only push people away. It was the threat of hell, not the mercy of God, that had initially sent me down that aisle of salvation, which meant that I was not yet saved.

The next morning, a fall breeze brushed through Honeymoon's wind chime, and Uncle Rat packed up his truck in silence. I was sad to see them go and sadder still that I had gotten Betty in trouble. I prayed to God for her to realize what I had only just learned that long, sad night—that it was love, not fear, that would save us.

Two Sundays later I got baptized. Baptisms were no longer held at the riverbank, as they had been when Pappy and Honeymoon met; now they took place at a small glass pool that had been built into the wall behind Saint Peter's choir box. For my big day Pappy had laid lush green plants all along the aisles and up the stairs to the pool. Pastor Green stood high in the pulpit, his black robe tucked inside his trousers protected by rubber knee boots. He opened the Bible and looked down at me repeating the words of John: "I baptize you with water, but He will baptize you with the Holy Spirit."

When the book was closed, the choir began to sing "Take Me to the Water," and a pair of ushers, clad in white, led me up to the pool where Pastor Green and Pappy, his deacon, were waiting. Pastor placed his right hand behind my head, which was wrapped tightly in a rubber cap and a long cloth. He raised his left hand up for the proclamation: "I baptize you, Yolanda Young, in the name of the Father, the Son, and the Holy Ghost." With that he clapped his left hand over my mouth and, with the help of Pappy, gently lowered me to the bottom of the square pool. I expected a cold shock, but the wetness was warm and comforting. When I rose, Pappy's face was the first I saw.

And Your Old Shall Dream Dreams

A dream comes when there are many cares.

—*Ecclesiastes 5:3*

One morning before marching off to work in heavy jeans and steel-toe boots, two of my uncles joined Big Momma and me for breakfast. At eight, I'd watched them devour a skillet of Jimmy Dean sausage and scrambled eggs many times, so only after they'd eaten three quarters of Big Momma's three-layer jelly cake was I impressed.

"Boys, remember how I use to love these here cakes?" she wondered, cupping her hands around a glass of prune juice. "I could cook one and then eat it all week with my breakfast. Then my sugar got bad and I couldn't eat 'em anymore."

"But you can still cook 'em, Big Momma," Uncle Wayne assured her after wiping his mouth.

"Exactly, son. Seeing you boys gnaw through one of my pound cakes just fills my soul. It's almost as good as eating 'em myself."

The young men, then in their early twenties, eyed their grandmother strangely, kissed her on the forehead, then made their way to work.

After waving them off from her front porch, unable to hold my tongue I asked, "Big Momma, what in the world was that all about?"

"More than cakes. Now, hush up," she said, swatting a fly. Later she made her slow way around offering me an explanation. And for the rest of the morning, and well into the evening, I listened with keen ears as Big Momma shared with me the dreams of my uncles.

She began by explaining that because so many of her hopes had flown away just like those robins that the boys tried to capture with their hands outside their back door, she felt it her job to teach them how to clamp on to a dream. She knew if desire ever left them, they'd soon be walking dead. Our neighborhood was filled with such hopeless men, so she was careful to always nourish the boys' appetites for life. Every time one of their dreams was dashed, Big Momma would care for her grandsons until they were strong enough to go after another one.

One only had to peek into the back room where my mother's brothers had grown up to know that they didn't stand much of a chance. While Uncle Rat rested on a cot in the living room, his six brothers slept in the back room side by side on two double mattresses, like shoes tucked into boxes—head, foot, head, foot, head, foot. The beds themselves filled the room almost to its leaning edges. Instead of building the room using levels and yardsticks, Pappy, who never had enough time with his long work hours, had simply nailed together a frame and covered it with wooden boards. The result was a sloped ceiling and drafty windows with rags stuffed in their cracks to keep out the cold.

Still air gathered between the mortared bricks holding up the house.

The room was dark, even during the summer, because backyard fruit trees and nearby houses hogged all the sunlight. And instead of using a coat of white paint to brighten it up, the boys had put up thin wall-sized sheets of pecan-colored plywood and called it paneling. To whisk away the pungent smell of musty armpits and feet, my uncles kept the back door open.

Stacked against one long shadowed wall were three brown dressers. Underneath the first, behind a few pairs of shoes, was a beer can's sawed-off bottom collecting the butts of cigarettes that the two older boys secretly smoked. Neatly displayed on the bureau's top were their boyhood tokens: a tall stack of paperback westerns, a pile of baseball cards, and, snug inside a Havana cigar box, a tobacco sack filled with marbles. The only thing the two of them didn't share was the pajamas that Honeymoon sewed from bolts of fabric she'd picked up for five cents a yard at G. C. Murphy. That dresser said everything about the two boys who shared it. They were close. They were resourceful. They were dreamers.

Baby Jane, or James as we called him when our tongues weren't lazy, was the older of the two, with Uncle Wayne falling two years behind him. Having been burdened with a girl's nickname, Baby Jane had grown up resilient. He had sad, sullen features that he often distorted while telling jokes that bowled us over with laughter. Uncle Wayne, known as Frog for the playful eyes that bulged from his head, did everything he could to avoid disappointment altogether. Since theirs was the house where the hungry came for a meal or to gather a basket of Pappy's tomatoes, peppers, and greens, my uncles had always been looked up to on the block. By their teenage years, the boys were considered handsome and well dressed in a way poor people admired. They wore neatly creased jeans with clean wide-collared shirts and walked with an air of confidence. Still, somehow impediments hovered over both of them wherever they went.

"When my senior year starts, we pulling up in our own car," Baby Jane had screeched one night from the top of the bed he shared with Uncle Wayne.

"Where we gon' get the money?" his brother asked, positioning himself so as not to taste feet.

"We gon' do what we do every summer—hustle," Baby Jane replied. "Only we can't blow the money."

Back then, hustling meant spending the hot summer selling empty bottles, mowing lawns, and beating their younger brothers at dominoes. Eventually they scrounged together enough dollar bills for the purchase of a '56 Plymouth. The car was fifteen years old, with a rusted hood and a muffler that dragged on the ground, but Big Momma extolled, "Boys, it's just beautiful. All it needs is some paint, a good polish and buff."

"But what about the seats?" Baby Jane had asked, looking through the window at the tears in the black leather.

"Don't worry. I can fix that." And she did by stitching heavy towels into seat covers. The boys painted the hot rod in their school's green and white and called it "the Viking" after the school mascot.

Although Baby Jane had supplied most of the money for the car, he was laid-back and generous about it. On the first day they took the Viking to school, he'd said to his brother, "Man, you drive and I'll ride. Tomorrow I'll take the wheel." Somehow, tomorrow never came. Baby Jane was just as happy daydreaming from the passenger side, especially on the day that he and his brother would compete in the state's baseball playoffs. None of the teammates' parents could afford to take a day off from cutting and scrubbing to watch their sons compete. But that didn't dull the boys' spirits, and they were still awarded a neighborhood prominence that spring. At church the Sunday before a big game, the pastor had offered a prayer for the team. Every night after baseball practice, the neighborhood boys would gather in the backyard to hear from Baby Jane what the coach had said, how the team was fielding, and if anyone really thought they could get a hit off of a tall, rubbery, and talented pitcher named Vida Blue.

"All we need is two," Baby Jane declared. "One hit gets us on base. Another brings us in. That lanky Blue can pitch, but everybody knows we're faster." Uncle Wayne nodded in agreement. Besides, there was more to gain than a championship. All season, major-league scouts had been filling the stands to watch Blue pitch. The Oakland Athletics had already made him its first pick, so now the scouts were coming to see what they'd be up against that summer. There was the chance that a scout might spot a Valencia player or two.

Big Momma recalled coming around to Honeymoon's to listen to Baby Jane use windups, umpire stands, and wide eyes to recount the game. With a wrinkled brow he began, "Man, everybody on that bus was excited on the way over to Mansfield. Butchy said he was gon' get him a hit, and I said I was gon' bring him in."

"But it wasn't to be, huh, boy?" asked Uncle Wayne, who had been handed Vida's last strikeout to end the game.

"Naw, man. I guess not. I knew the moment that old lanky boy threw his first pitch across the plate that he had it today."

While Baby Jane went on talking he must have known instinctively that Uncle Wayne was wondering if any of the scouts had seen him, because he tapped his younger brother on the shoulder and said with assurance, "Wayne, your time gon' come."

Baby Jane had always known that he wasn't that good a pitcher, but he knew the game and could talk his teammates into playing their hearts out. His first love had actually been football, but he was thinner than a corn husk. When he was fourteen, Baby Jane tried out for the team to show the neighborhood boys that he could do anything they could.

"No, precious baby," Honeymoon had told her son. "You leave that for the bigger boys." It was a frequent exchange— Honeymoon trying to save Baby Jane from detriment, her son unable to heed her warning. Big Momma saw value in his learning the lesson for himself, so when Baby Jane ran to her front porch where she was busy stripping sticky peas from their hulls, she just said, "Sounds good to me, son. Go show 'em what you got."

After the first day of practice, Baby Jane limped home. The second day he was carried. By the third day, there was no more talk of football. The same occurred after that day of pitching against Blue. Whipped and defeated, Baby Jane took the passenger seat once again, deciding to live his baseball dream through his younger brother.

"You're the one with the pure swing and quickness," he said, reassuringly.

"We'll see," Uncle Wayne answered in a quiet voice. Inside, he hoped that Baby Jane was right.

For the last few years of high school, Baby Jane had been fostering another dream, one he thought well within his grasp. Mr. Ellis, a pudgy, kindhearted teacher, had been the first to suggest to Baby Jane that he set his sights on being the first in his family to go away to college. Baby Jane sat back and imagined himself in a cardigan sweater and glasses, with an armful of books and a pretty girl at his side. When Big Momma caught wind of Mr. Ellis's suggestion, she never missed an occasion to remind Baby Jane of his college dream and for good measure threw in, "And how 'bout becoming a lawyer? Just like that Perry Mason."

The boys never stopped to evaluate a dream for its plausibility. Had they done that, they would never have ventured beyond their back room, so while Baby Jane set off to Southern University in Baton Rouge with a couple of pillowcases filled with clothes, linens, and enough money to purchase his political science books, Uncle Wayne got back to their baseball dream. A few recruiters had seen enough in his performance against Vida Blue to know he was "one to watch," and by the end of his junior year, Uncle Wayne was certain if he kept it up, he'd have a scholarship or maybe even get drafted into the majors.

Before any of that could happen, fate stepped in. Nearly twenty years had passed since the Supreme Court outlawed segregation in *Brown* v. *Board of Education of Topeka*, but white officials in Louisiana used the legal tactic of state interposition, as well as harassment, to keep its black children out of white schools. To end segregation for good, the Supreme Court stepped in again and demanded that Louisiana school boards immediately employ every method available to them to integrate its schools. Unfortunately for Uncle Wayne, the decree became effective on the first day of March. Instead of driving the Viking to baseball practice, Uncle Wayne took the school bus to a white school called Byrd High.

"It'll be all right, precious baby" was all his mother, Honeymoon, could say to reassure him. Next to her, draped in a floral apron, Big Momma offered more. "Now, boy, you go over to that school and you don't give them no trouble, but you don't take no mess either. I'm gon' sit in my window chair right next to the phone, waiting to come up there at the first hint of trouble."

There wasn't much Big Momma could have done. Still, Uncle Wayne found her words comforting as he boarded the school bus with his black classmates, all of them wondering what the new school would be like. In some ways, the transition was better than he had expected. No one pushed him in the halls, and the word "nigger" seeped out only a few times. Whenever possible, black teachers taught black students. In the rare instances when white teachers were forced to address integrated classes, they tried to set a tone.

"I don't know how you people are used to acting, but you will behave in here or find yourself outside that door," one teacher shouted, visibly angry.

Uncle Wayne had a shorter fuse than Baby Jane and found it difficult to remember his place. For instance, when Baby Jane left for college, Uncle Wayne inherited his Saturday lawns— one of which belonged to Mr. Mims, an ornery old white man who expected his lawn boy, for a fee of five dollars, to spend a minimum of three hours cutting, clipping, and trimming his large yard. Mr. Mims was not at all pleased to find Uncle Wayne washing his hands with the hose, declaring himself finished after only forty minutes.

"Well, you're not getting five dollars then," Mr. Mims said, shoving three crinkled bills into Uncle Wayne's clean, manicured hand.

"Look, Mr. Mims," Uncle Wayne said, looking straight at him, "I get paid by the job, not the hour. Now I cut your grass, edged the sidewalks and driveway, and trimmed the hedges. I ain't got all day to be here with you, so just give me my other two dollars."

Uncle Wayne wasn't quite risking a lynching, though some bad could have surely come to him, but after a long pause Mr. Mims handed over the two dollars and told Uncle Wayne to come earlier the following week.

Now Uncle Wayne faced down his English teacher with the same defiance. "Why did you just talk to us like that?" he asked her, characteristically smoothing away the crinkles in his shirt. "Have we done anything wrong? Do you think we want to be here?"

Embarrassed, the young white woman turned and faced the chalkboard.

Uncle Wayne had always found the words to take up for himself—until the day of his first Byrd High baseball game, when his coach refused to play him. The same way the school had refused to allow Valencia's black cheerleaders to join Byrd's squad.

"This ain't football, boy," his coach said. "Baseball's a white man's game."

Uncle Wayne was at first speechless and then despondent. But when the black kids all got together and pledged to walk out, Uncle Wayne was one of the first through the door. It seemed clear there was no liberty or equality at Byrd, so they assembled under the flagpole. In truth, it was the only place where they still felt they had some dignity, and they refused to go back inside. Not a lot of time had been given to organizing the walkout. The Stoner Hill teenagers had decided on their bus ride home the day before to leave the building during lunch. The black students who hadn't managed to hear about it just got swept up in the emotional wave and drifted outside with the others.

Big Momma said her heart almost stopped when she caught wind of what had happened. As soon as word reached her late in the day, she rushed over to the boys' back door to hear the whole story from Uncle Wayne.

"The principal called that evil old D'Artois," Uncle Wayne said, pronouncing the police commissioner's name "Doortoy," with a familiar disdain. D'Artois was hated around our parts because of his meanness. It was said that for Friday-night amusement, he made the city's three black police officers beat up any black man who dared to stumble out of the Cobra Club a little tipsy.

"Yeah," Uncle Wayne continued, sitting on the back step with a bitter look on his face, "they got scared seeing all that black outside their school doors. I guess they thought we were gon' burn the city down like folks did in Los Angeles after King got killed."

When D'Artois first got there, he just leaned against his police car watching the dusky crowd through his sunglasses. Then he pulled his wide-brimmed hat down and started walking slowly toward them while whipping the sweat off of his fat neck.

"When he reached the flagpole, he did like this," Uncle Wayne said, and gestured as though he was adjusting his belt buckle and pulling up his pants. "Then he yelled at us, 'Who's leading this thing?' When no one stepped forward, I was sure he was gon' call out the dogs."

The walkout had no leader or structured plan. It had occurred like a gas leak—first there is just a fleeting whiff in the air, then the smell grows pungent, and finally comes the explosion. In a way, though, the seeping had begun more than a decade earlier, when Dr. Martin Luther King, Jr., had come to our dusty town to speak of equality and human rights at the Galilee Baptist Church. Over the years that followed, white retribution occurred by way of front-yard cross burnings, church bombings, and a few lynchings in a nearby town. During the early sixties, D'Artois showed the power of his wrath by ordering the beating of the Reverend Harry Blake after blacks marched in a peaceful civil-rights march down Milam Street. For some time the two sides, black and white, battled each other. Now even D'Artois had grown tired. Neither side wanted any trouble.

"We just wanted some respect," Uncle Wayne explained to Big Momma.

"Lord have mercy, boy. That crazy white man could've killed you," Big Momma said, and puckered her lips as though she'd tasted something sour. Some teachers continued with their lesson plans and others surrendered teaching, fixing their eyes on the standoff outside. Mr. Ellis, one of the black teachers brought over from Valencia, was the only one brave enough to join the students.

"This is peaceful, sir," he pleaded in his quiet, patient way. Mr. Ellis shared D'Artois's stocky build, but nothing else. Still, he knew the chief was the kind of white man who expected blacks to talk to him a certain way. "These young men and women are just hurt and broken. They gave up their school, their class offices, their prom and graduation to be here. Now they've come to find out they aren't a part of this new school."

The commissioner considered Mr. Ellis's words, pulling his collar away from his neck. "Well," he said in a drawl like the idling motor on a diesel truck, "we gon' get all this settled, but y'all got to go back to class right now." In the end, the redneck officer only created further division by arranging a separate black prom and allowing the black graduates to wear Valencia's green-and-white robes.

The experience left Uncle Wayne bitter and hopeless, but Big Momma reminded him about the college coach who'd called him several times, following Valencia's run in the baseball playoffs, urging him to keep in touch. Big Momma made Uncle Wayne give the man a call. "I remember you, son," the coach said to him. "Come on down. I'd love to see what you've got."

Just when things were getting back on track for Uncle Wayne, Big Momma reminded me of the dream she'd gone and had.

I was five that summer and was lying next to Big Momma when she got up from her dream. It was early, before dawn, even before Miss Gustavia's rooster had stretched his neck and cleared his throat. Big Momma moved suddenly, and the springs in her mattress cried out, startling me awake.

"Big Momma, whatcha doing?" I asked her. Ignoring me, she leaned out of her maple bed and turned on the table lamp. The light burned my eyes as I stared up at the glowing white ceiling and listened to the chime of the ceiling fan as it whirled the smell of Ben-Gay through the room. I asked again, "A nightmare?"

"Hush up, girl," she said then. "I been wrestling with this dream all night long. You go back to sleep."

I closed my eyes to feign obedience but quickly reopened them to find Big Momma kneeling beside her bed. In front of her was a small table holding her leather-bound Bible. She fanned back the pages until she reached the concordance, which she used to lead her when she was presented with life's uncertainties. She thumbed down, using her crooked index finger as a guide. When she fell upon the word "dream," she stilled herself and mumbled, *"And he dreamed yet another dream."*

As she spoke, I slowly pulled the covers over my head. We were raised on Big Momma's visions. They could be about something as simple as a swimming fish signifying a forth-coming pregnancy or a plate missing from the table warning of an impending death. Either way, the family had come to antici-pate their fulfillment.

Big Momma continued reading through her Scriptures. *"What is this dream that thou hast dreamt. . . . And your old shall dream dreams. . . . For a dream cometh when there are many cares. . . . And the dream is certain."*

"Big Momma, what did you dream?" I begged to know. She looked at me heavily and for a long time. Then she answered, "It was two dreams really, one with a young man in a deep blue suit digging small seashells out of the sand by cold water. The other one had the same boy in it, only he was running from a fire that was catching up to him."

Big Momma stayed bent, first praying the Our Father. Then came more Scripture readings, then a prayer for understand-ing, and another for discernment and another for peace and another for persuasion and another and another and another. Comfort didn't return to her bones until she pulled herself up by the acorn carvings that capped the bedposts.

"That boy is 'bout to be drafted to war," she whispered to her-self.

Big Momma had been given the dream, but it was Uncle Wayne who had the vision. Many of his friends had been drafted, so he knew that for him it was just a matter of time. Enough of them had come back mangled or dead for him to know that he didn't want to go. He had just enough hope saved up to believe that he could find a way out. Soon after Big Momma's dream, Uncle Wayne got a call from an Air Force recruiter. "Did you know," the officer asked, "we can train you in office procurement and you won't have to go to Vietnam?"

Several weeks later Uncle Wayne's draft notice arrived, but he was already gone. A few days earlier, he'd put on a navy blue Air Force uniform and been flown to Seattle, where a gray ocean washed the seashells of Big Momma's dream up along the shore. Uncle Wayne never called that college coach again and never said whether he was relieved or pained to have traded his dream of playing baseball for one that saved his life.

Comforted that Uncle Wayne was safe, Baby Jane continued with college, with less than two years remaining. The following semester's tuition money, earned from a summer of planting trees, sat in a shoe box underneath Honeymoon's bed. The day after Thanksgiving, Baby Jane took the money with him back to school. A relative with whom he was riding suggested they take a slight detour to New Orleans for the Bayou Classic football game.

Our cousin Sleek was a jackleg preacher who, in the spirit of Elmer Gantry, knew how to lull the innocent, the weary, and, in the case of Baby Jane, the loquacious down a treacherous road. Once trapped, Sleek chewed them up the way a cow would cud. Knowing this, his mother had cautioned Baby Jane against going anywhere with Sleek.

"He's no good, I tell you," she said, recounting the times Sleek had stopped in her home for a visit and for the sole purpose of lifting something. It didn't matter how trite it was. He'd steal a filthy ashtray. Baby Jane, being headstrong, didn't heed her warning. "I'm grown, m'dear," he'd replied, indignant. "I can take care of myself."

During the five-hour drive from Shreveport to New Orleans,

Sleek had time to uncover every secret that Baby Jane possessed, from the amount of his savings to the state of his romance. He started with a simple question: "So whatcha doing with yourself these days?"

"Well," Baby Jane said in a thoughtful and serious manner, "I'm pledging Alpha Phi Alpha this coming semester, and Dawn wants to get married after we graduate."

"*Ssmeeeeek.*" Sleek sucked his teeth, and added sarcastically, "Pledging and getting married, you a big-time man."

"Oh, yeah," Baby Jane said, smiling.

"How much money it takes to do all that?" Sleek needed to know.

"At least a few thousand, but I got it. Don't worry about me."

"How long you been dating that girl?"

"Off and on about three years, but it's getting serious now."

"Serious, *smeeeek*? I don't know what the hell that smart pretty girl sees in yo' ugly self."

"Neither do I, but I'm going with it."

They bantered until they reached New Orleans, where Sleek pulled up to the Grand Hyatt Hotel adjacent to the Superdome. He said a big man should stay at a big-time hotel.

"Suites for each of us," Sleek told the desk clerk, then leaned over to a distressed-looking Baby Jane. "Don't worry, son. This is on me."

Later Sleek asked, "What did you bring to wear to the game?"

Baby Jane produced his suit, tailored by the neighborhood seamstress, and Sleek sucked his teeth dismissively at the sight of it. The blue polyester jacket was a slim-fitting box cut that buttoned up like a shirt and matched the slightly flared slacks. Shiny navy blue shoes with gold trim completed the ensemble.

"Boy, we got to get you some new clothes for the weekend,"

Sleek said, giving no reason for his disapproval. Off they went to an exclusive men's clothing store. Baby Jane had only heard of the store, but Sleek acted as though he paid the tailor's salary himself. He picked out a nice two-piece leisure suit for Baby Jane and a three-piece silk-and-wool blend for himself. They bought shirts, ties, and a couple of sweaters for the chilly night air. At the register Sleek's credit card was rejected.

"Take care of it, boy," Sleek said. "I'll get you back later."

By game time the next morning, after a night of partying and the purchase of upgraded stadium suite seats, a nagging anxiety was setting in Baby Jane's mind. Not even the sight of Grambling State's legendary coach, Eddie Robinson, could snap him out of his funk. As Southern University's marching band formed the game score on the field, Baby Jane could think of nothing but how he'd wasted the contents of his now empty shoe box and tossed it on the front seat of Sleek's car.

Baby Jane finished the semester, then came home for Christmas and was depressed to find that all his gifts—some pens, a briefcase, and a piece of leather luggage—would have been useful were he planning to return to school. There was no chance for him to get that money back in time. Hardly able to keep food on the table and meet the seventy-two-dollar-a-month mortgage, the family could do nothing to help Baby Jane, so they responded to his shattered dream the way they would a deformity: they looked away with compassion and sadness. Sleek didn't come around for some time, and even when he did, Baby Jane never got his money back.

"It's just a little setback is all," Big Momma assured him. "You can work this spring with your pappy and go back to school next year." But Baby Jane never went back. Instead he got a job on the railroad cracking steel tracks with an iron hammer, the sun burning his eyes all day while sweat collected like rain in his boots.

Baby Jane had been working for the railroad almost three years when Wayne returned from the Air Force looking for a job. Naturally they ended up working on the railroad together. Big Momma thought that was fine enough, but still she insisted, "You gotta have a dream."

Somehow Baby Jane and Uncle Wayne had understood what Big Momma's question about jelly cakes had really meant. Over the weeks that followed, the two of them bumped their heads together. They wrote down plans on Big Momma's kitchen table, made phone calls, and went door to door. They'd started late but had decided not to wait any longer. The Stoner Hill Tigers baseball team debuted the first week of July. That first summer league was little more than the kids from the neighborhood wearing red-and-blue T-shirts playing against each other, but as Big Momma saw it, there was no better way to feed the soul than to give someone else a dream to hold.

Strawberries in July

The remains of a forest enfolded Stoner Hill. The heart of it
grew unattended just across the street from Honeymoon's
house. Sycamore trees and fat Southern cottonwood poplars
leaned into one another and listened as the mockingbirds sang.
The goosenecked pines peered out over the grove. Dirt paths
wound through the trees. Scattered among them were red
catkins, green pecans, and striped saucer-shaped acorns. Beyond this lay an open field, fringed with berry bushes.

On days when the sun was being shy, I'd sit on the hood of
Pappy's boring brown Pinto and stare at those woods, daunted
by their darkness. Sometimes my mother's youngest brothers
would come swinging their naked ashy feet and join me while
their soggy canvas sneakers dried on the fence. On their laps
they'd balance large, lime green Tupperware bowls containing

the spoils of their venture into the forest and the cause of my envy. From the bowls they carelessly scooped fistfuls of leaking strawberries and shoved them into the backs of their mouths. Hardly bothering to chew, they seemed to just swallow the berries whole.

They'd pick the berries from the bushes and, while still hot in their hands, wash them with the water hose. Some days the varmints would steal sugar from the old mayonnaise jar in the kitchen and sprinkle it all over the berries until they crystallized into red candy. Other times the berries' own juice was sweet enough to satisfy. My uncles would never share with me because they were like that—the grouch, Michael, and the philosopher, Donny, each in his own way trying to teach me a lesson: if I was too afraid to venture into the woods, they reasoned, I didn't deserve to share in the fruits of their labor. But I knew that deep down, they felt sorry for me.

When I was around the age of eight or nine, my fifteen-year-old uncle, Michael, decided to take matters into his own hands, declaring to me, "I killed the mutt yesterday, shot him dead in the neck with my BB gun, so you can go on in the woods." The grouch knew it wasn't the trails themselves that I feared, it was the half-wild dogs that roamed them.

"That was Mr. Smith's dog you killed," I responded tartly. "You're not getting me to go in them woods."

"Yolanda, you have nothing to fear but fear itself," Donny quoted.

"Whatever, boy," I interrupted. Otherwise, I'd have to listen to him talk all day.

"I'll go with you, girl," Michael said, laughing at me. "You know I won't let no dog get to you." It was true—the grouch had earned my trust a few years earlier when he'd taught me to ride

my bike that I'd christened Scorpio. I hadn't wanted him to remove the training wheels for fear of tumbling catastrophes, but
my uncle faithfully ran barefoot beside me, panting, "Londa,
don't say you're gonna fall. 'Cause then you will. When you feel
like you're losing control, ring the bell and I'll steady you."
From that day on I wobbled but never fell while riding down
our bumpy street.

Still, I shook my head fiercely now at his suggestion that I
trust him to guard me in the forest. But Michael knew he could
change my mind.

"Come on!" he barked gruffly, jumping from the car. "Go get
a bowl." Slowly, I followed behind him.

I had been scared of dogs, cats, and even rabbits—any furred,
unpredictable creature—since my second birthday, when Aunt
Doll, wearing a wig and a shapeless brown skirt, presented me
with a trembling, red-eyed bunny. At the sight of it everything
seemed to jump from my body—veins popped from my neck,
hair shot up on my head, cries flew from my mouth, and pee
cascaded down my culottes.

Long after the cottontail had vanished, my terror lingered.
One winter morning, I happened on Pappy's hunting bounty of
possum, raccoon, and squirrel skins hanging from the porch.
The meat had already been cut out and cured for sausage.
Pappy would later stuff some of the skins and make a new hat
from others, but not before I swore a dozen times over that their
remains, their startled eyes and brisk tails swinging in the
breeze, were taunting me.

Concerned that my fear would lead me to harm, Honeymoon
determined to break me of it. She instructed Michael and
Donny to lock me in their rusty hands, then untied her puppy
and rubbed him all over my face, arms, and legs. As the dog

licked at my body, Honeymoon said, "See, Londa, he won't hurt you." Those were the last words I heard before passing out. After that, Honeymoon gave up trying.

Heading toward the woods with my own Tupperware bowl, I was stopped by the memory of that dog's sandy wet tongue.

"You can't change your mind," Michael railed. I dropped to the ground and caught hold of the fence as he tried to drag me.

"Let her go, Michael," Donny yelled. Then to me he said flatly, "You'll never be able to go to Paris for the simple fact that you too afraid of everything."

"Paris?" Michael and I repeated in a fleeting moment of confused solidarity.

"You never been to Beaumont, Texas, let alone Paris," Michael said, trying to make Donny feel stupid.

"I know about Paris," Donny assured us. "That's where Richard Wright and James Baldwin went to write. I'm gon' be like those brothers, a black man writing in Paris. I'm leaving here as soon as I graduate." Donny, a high school senior, was looking forward to enlisting in the Air Force the following year.

"You don't even understand the way they talk over there," Michael said, waving Donny off.

"And are you sure there're black people in Paris?" I asked in disbelief.

Donny shot us a disgusted look. "Listen. All I'm saying is that people around here never went anywhere and never done anything for the simple fact they scared to move, scared to even look around the corner. But I ain't scared."

"Well, I ain't scared to go neither," I said, my fingers disfiguring my plastic bowl.

Donny looked at me with one side of his mouth still twisted in judgment. "When Wayne was stationed in Germany, he wrote me a letter and said he'd taken a bus trip to Paris and in all the restaurants and cafés (that's what they call bakeries) and even the grocery stores, people would bring their dogs in with them."

"What?" I said. "That's crazy and nasty. I don't believe you."

"Believe it, kid. You'd piss your pants."

"Yeah, Yolanda," Michael chimed in. "You too scared to go across the street. How you gon' go to Paris?"

When he was twelve, Donny had taken a piece of particleboard the size of a door and, using the encyclopedia, sketched out the world on it. He glued on an assortment of dried beans to represent each continent, then painted the sections different colors. After it won first prize at the social studies fair, Honeymoon hung the picture in the living room. When some of the peas started to fall off, she remounted the picture outside on the porch. Donny suddenly turned around to look at it.

"This is where we are, Yolanda," he said, running up and pointing at the red stain that represented the potbellied United States. "And here's where you'll never go." Sweeping his finger up over all the shapes and colors between Louisiana and Paris, he called out the states one by one. "That's Mississippi, Alabama, Georgia," and on until he reached New York. Then his hand took a giant leap over the blue lima beans that represented the waves of the Atlantic Ocean and dropped his finger down on a gold blot. "And this is Paris. The place you'll never see."

"But I'm going," I snarled through my teeth. "But you going with me," I said pulling Uncle Michael into the street. My feet sank into the loamy soil where the forest began to spread its roots. The dirt and growing things smelled sweet. The place was an overwhelming world of its own with blue jays hopping from one branch to another, leaves shaking themselves from branches, and yawning openings in tree trunks. I saw several potato-chip and gum wrappers left, I imagined, by fearless children. A faded rag that looked to have been red at some point seemed to crawl out of the ground. I could tell from all the footprints—some showing the arch of bare feet, others with track ridges, and even some high-heel punctures—that many feet had trodden these paths.

"Londa, come on." Michael looked back, jerking his arm away from me while snapping fallen twigs with his bare feet. "The dogs don't need to hear you. They can smell your scaredy butt."

"Oh, God. I see one coming," I called while Michael looked around. "He's over there," I said, pointing to a prowling fur hide. My senses sharpened with fear. I knew their sour smells, the patterns of their coats, and their sounds, from a throaty murmur to a vicious growl. I could sense them before I could see them: a man walking in a constricted fashion was probably holding a leash; a moving shadow or rustling leaves warned of a cat on foot; a changing wind pattern or chinking noise was a clue that something quiet but ferocious was brushing past. My fear had become like blindness; I saw things with my ears and with my skin.

I ran toward the berry patches, and the dog, attracted by my movement, followed, barking, but Michael cut him off and swung at him with a tree limb. I burst into the yellow-green sunlight and spit up relief. With the smile of a battle won, I looked over the fruit plants.

"Don't pick the hard green ones, Londa."

"I know." Just because I'd never picked them didn't mean I hadn't sneaked enough of them to know which ones were good. I plucked the berries so quickly that my skin tore on their stems.

When not another strawberry would fit into my bowl, I looked up from the low-sprawling green leaves and spotted a light brown dog with a stumpy tail walking at the edge of the woods.

Michael left off picking his own berries and called out, "Okay, Londa. I'll scare him off. You run." And I did. With one arm wrapped around my bowl and the other forming a cage over my precious fruit, I made it back to the sunlight and into the gate of Honeymoon's house. Michael came up behind me, and we leaned against the Pinto to catch our breath.

"You have conquered your fear, Yolanda," Donny said, stretching his hands out to me.

"Not really," I said while placing my shoes on the fence with the others. I carefully took a warm berry from my bowl and dropped it whole into my mouth. Its delicate hairs brushed against my teeth while sweet and tart juices ran across my tongue. My heart had not yet slowed down, and my fingers, bruised during my battle, were starting to burn. Still, the taste of that first strawberry stayed with me.

The Party Line

The words of a gossip are like choice morsels; they go down
to the inmost parts of the belly.

—*Proverbs 18:8*

As a young child, my greatest pleasure was not watching TV
but resting on the floor at the feet of adults, listening unobtru-
sively while they passed around stories. I remember watching
Big Momma jerk forward, a black rotary phone pressed tightly
against her ear. "What you say, girl?" Then, after a long pause,
"Hush yo' mouth." Big Momma had her "people" who kept her
informed. Likewise, she returned the favor. They called it the
party line because word on any topic would travel from the bus
stop through the neighborhood between the church pews and
back again much the way phone lines behave when the wiring
gets crossed up.

Momma's baby sister, Ruby (a surprise that accompanied
Honeymoon's change in life), and I would feign interest in a
silent game of checkers, all the while absorbing our mothers'
words. Later we would recount the rumors, Ruby relaying the

particulars, me nodding to back her up. When she wanted to crack me up, my aunt would sit in Big Momma's high-back chair, throw her head back on the lace doily, and mimic Big Momma's short "a-hoo" laugh.

Ruby enjoyed spinning tales. Jokes, lies, and gossip flowed from her lips like drippings from an ice cream cone. Sometimes she'd catch the excess, recalling a story verbatim, but more often she added details as she went along. Usually no one quibbled over her minor alterations, but every so often those fabrications made a mess of everything.

The rumor mill was active in Stoner Hill, not because the people there were spiteful or mean-spirited but because often they were bored. Every day was the same: homemade biscuits and eggs for breakfast, work in kitchens or factories, greens and ham hocks for dinner, and afterward church or TV, then bed. There was so little to do that once when Jimmy Carter was president, our school let us out early just to watch his motorcade drive down the street. So naturally we welcomed the stories that leavened the dull day. The neighborhood reared up for only three things—the annual church musical, shotgun blasts on New Year's Eve, and the Miss Valencia Junior High Pageant—and even on these occasions stories flew the way moss grew, fast and thick.

The pageant—a parade of glitter-coated felt capes and twirling baton sticks—was a rite of passage for popular girls in Stoner Hill. It had been a long time since Momma's pageant victory, and Honeymoon had waited longer than it takes a puppy to grow old for another girl of hers to wear that crown. Ruby entered the pageant when she was in the seventh grade, and she intended to win it. When my aunt fixed her mind on a thing, she was like a sprung rat trap, unwilling to let go.

The pageant chair was the school's music director, Mr. Bud. From the first day of rehearsals, Ruby sensed that Mr. Bud showed a preference for a contestant named Kenya Jefferson, a pimply faced girl who thought very highly of herself. "He treats her like she's his daughter or something," Ruby complained. "And he acts like it's a foregone conclusion that she's gon' be the next Miss Valencia."

At practice one afternoon Ruby's radar caught a glitter in Mrs. Jefferson's eye as she passed Mr. Bud in the aisle, and her mouth snapped shut on another idea: Kenya's momma and Mr. Bud must be—no, were—in an intimate relationship. Ruby's turned-up nose whiffed something foul. Under normal circumstances such a discovery would have amused her, but now it seemed to place her crown in jeopardy—Mr. Bud selected the judges to score the contestants.

As Ruby recounted the details of the "Kenya affair," I recalled the last time I'd seen her this mad. She was ten and pissed that some girls had swindled six-year-old me. I had found her reared back in Pappy's recliner like an emperor waiting to hear a pauper's lame excuse about why there was no tribute for him. During my story, she scratched her big toe, which poked out of her left sock, and never looked away from the TV clown humiliating contestants with showers of confetti and bangs on a metal gong.

Earlier that lazy afternoon, while taking a break from propelling our bikes along the river levee, Ruby had volunteered me to go buy sweets at the neighborhood store. Stocked with most of the necessities—sardines, toilet tissue, cough drops, and some candy jewels we wore like they were the real thing—the two-room shack with its back-porch bathroom was owned by a gargantuan woman who smelled like pickled pigs' feet.

Because she harbored an arrested body and a marble eye, she left the task of manning the store to her nieces, the Pette twins.

Although Momma insisted that I never use the words "black" and "ugly" in unison, these twelve-year-old girls were ugly and as black as a December night, both of them in six feet of skin as rough as tree bark. Sneaky as weasels, they schemed money from customers by giving the wrong change or shorting them on a purchase. That day for a dollar, I was to have gotten two packs of M&M's, four rolls of Sweetarts, a box of Lemonheads, a pack of Kool-Aid, and some change. Instead, they had dropped a few empty candy boxes into my bag along with a smashed candy bar and ten noisy pennies. I was almost home when I checked the bag and realized that I'd been cheated.

When I told Ruby what happened, predictably, she was as angry as a kicked bull, and we went back to the store.

"Y'all owe us some change," my aunt demanded, twisting the words out the side of her mouth. Her jaws were locked, ready for battle. One of the twins, Stacey, knew enough to lie low. "Give it to her, Tracey," she urged her sister.

"I don't know whatchoo talkin' 'bout," Tracey yelled from across the counter.

"Well, you gon' find out, or I'm whipping your ass today," Ruby growled.

The glass-eyed lady tried to rise up then. "You better get on outta here, gurl." Ruby shot her a look, and she shut back up. When Tracey refused to surrender my money, Ruby went diving headfirst over the counter, her sandals parting company with her feet in midflight and her panties flashing like a caution signal from below her skirt. I stood back in awe as she mixed it up, grabbing Tracey's neck and pushing her into a wall. The shelf behind them dropped half its load of Vienna sausages and Twinkies to the floor, on its way delivering a nice lump to Tracey's forehead. Stacey and I stared at each other, hoping neither of us would jump into the ring. I didn't. There was no need.

Minutes later, when we emerged from the dim interior of that store out into the smothering Southern heat, Ruby looked down at her arm, sliced open by a nail, and smiled, our returned money hot in her damp hand.

Everyone in the neighborhood caught wind of the incident, and it became the cornerstone of Ruby lore. Now, two years later, her wrath awaited Kenya. Instead of employing tussle methods, the aspiring queen refined her technique, intending to smack Kenya by shaming her. One by one Ruby snatched up each contestant's ear. In Cynthia's she poured the bit about "Mrs. Jefferson rubbing her chest against Mr. Bud, who smiled and licked his lips." To Jeneane she confided what we'd spied from the top of the levee—a garbage fire blazing at one end of the neighborhood and evidence of the teacher and parent heating up the other. To Tammy she pointed out that Mr. Bud's car was parked in front of Kenya's house one night.

Girls of twelve and thirteen often spoke with maturity, so it was easy for adults to forget they were only children. This was the case with the pageant mothers who fed on their daughters' bits of information. By the night of the pageant, it was all anyone was talking about.

Because Valencia's auditorium doubled as the school's cafeteria, it smelled of onions and ammonia. Its cinder-block walls, painted the drab gray of a metal toolbox, rose up twenty or more feet and caused conversations to echo through the rafters, making it easy to pick up other conversations. "Sista, the winner of this pageant's already been decided," I heard Mrs. Watson say from her seat a few rows up from us, with her hand cupped over her friend's ear.

Through clenched teeth, the postman's wife replied, "You ain't telling me nothing. My husband called that a long time ago."

Their chatter was interrupted by Mr. Bud's slurred introduction of the contestants. "Mary Lou . . . Cynthia . . . Keeenya . . ."

"Mr. Bud must've taken him a sip before he came out," my uncle Michael joked to his brothers.

"Yep," Donny replied. "He's still hitting the bottle."

"Who? Who?" I begged to know.

The lady next to me, hiding under a wide-brimmed hat, pointed toward the stage. "That man up there," she said. "I can smell the beer from here."

The girls paraded out in cotton prairie-style dresses with wide lace collars and flared skirts. Despite Mr. Bud's attempts to the contrary, Ruby had worked her way up to being the pageant's star, the one chosen to shout, "Brick House!" as the girls danced to a popular Commodores song.

She nailed down the talent competition with a sassy rendition of Natalie Cole's "I'm Catching Hell" but looked more like she was giving hell—lips tight, eyes red—when Kenya still somehow managed to take home that Miss Valencia Junior High School crown, outscoring Ruby by a point.

It was a bittersweet victory for Kenya. As she promenaded up and down the aisles, patting tears and mascara from her joyful eyes, she noticed that few people smiled back. The rumor had done its work. Many gave knowing sneers and whispered as she passed. Before her lonely walk was ended, she had begun to cry with embarrassment.

Of course someone eventually told Kenya what Ruby had

done, and Kenya waited to return the favor. Ruby was easy prey. She had a crazy streak, a hot temper, and was in every way fast. With tree switches for legs, she grabbed one first-place track ribbon after another, only to dash behind the concession stand to share a cigarette with another runner or smooch with some boy. Because my aunt was always doing something shocking, it was easy to keep up scuttlebutt about her, and when she heard one of these stories, she only grinned. "What's the point?" she'd say to me. "There's always gon' be back-fence talk."

But the rumors had always been innocent, not affecting her life much one way or the other. Then one day, not long after the pageant, Ruby started getting pains in her stomach, so severe they caused her to jerk in a seizure and sometimes pass out. The first time it happened she was in the school cafeteria. She ended up wrapped in a ball under the table. Pappy and Honeymoon took her to the emergency room at the public hospital, where they waited all day in a hot, crowded reception area for a bunch of tests that uncovered nothing. At school the next day, Ruby heard the rumors—"You know that girl has always been touched" and "That wild girl is just trying to get some attention"—but Kenya sparked the best tale of them all. Leaning over the long white lunch table, with heads turned to her like cats to a bowl of milk, the rebuffed queen whispered what she claimed to have heard: "Please save my baby."

Ruby had another fit that afternoon at the water fountain, then another two days later on the floor of the girls' locker room. She couldn't take the pain. At home I rubbed her back as she lay in a ball on the bathroom floor. I was scared Ruby was going to die, and so when Kenya's little sister, Shanon, teased me on the playground about Ruby's "condition," I didn't hesitate in administering a few lashes across her face and neck. I grabbed that little girl and pulled her down under a thicket of trees where Spanish moss was collecting. To divert my licks, she flung out her arms like a drowning dog, and birds scattered in all directions. I swung at Shanon with my eyes closed. She moved, and instead of landing on her, my fist went through the soft moss and into a gum tree. I untangled my hand and discovered that both my knuckles and Shanon's face were bleeding. Our recess teacher rushed over and demanded to know why we were fighting. I explained it all to her—how while Shanon thought she was innocently teasing me, my aunt was really hurting. I was trying to choke off the gossip the way the moss had stunted that tree's fruit. My teacher shook her head at me impatiently and delivered the standard line: "That's senseless, Yolanda. People are going to talk."

The doctors finally discovered what had been ailing Ruby. It wasn't her stomach at all; rather, she had an impacted bowel. After several enemas, Ruby was back and once again we were spreading rumors. We treated the lies the way we did roaches, trying to stomp out the ones that got out of hand but always knowing there were more between the floor cracks.

Musical Chairs

The race is not to the swift or the battle to the strong, nor does
food come to the wise or wealth to the brilliant or favor to the
learned; but time and chance happen to them all.

—*Ecclesiastes 9:11*

Stoner Hill Elementary School comprised six narrow rows of
red-brick buildings lined up together like cars in a train yard.
The structures were connected by wide sidewalks covered
overhead with heavy tin roofs, which provided protection from
the sun and frequent rainstorms but could also raise the pitch
of hundreds of young voices into one continuous, echoing roar.
Every weekday—even in summers, thanks to a government
program providing for year-round lunch—I walked at a slow
and easy pace in a long line that meandered from one end of
the school to the cafeteria. I usually walked behind my best
friend, Laura Fitzpatrick, or Fizz, as everyone called her on account of her last name and because her skin was the delicious
color of a root beer float. Those in front and back of us would
call one another to look at her because Fizz was beautiful. She

was thin, but in a wiry rather than a waifish way; gold hair held together at the top of her head by elastic and plastic yellow balls swayed in the wind like the silky tail on a pony. Mostly, the kids gawked at her because she looked nothing like the rest of us.

On one such occasion, following the sounds of music, laughter, and moving chairs, Fizz and I poked our heads into a classroom to find children much younger than we were playing a game we were taught in Head Start, musical chairs. As anyone knew, all our game required was four pancake-colored chairs, five participants who made a circle around them, and a song. The little ones danced around the chairs singing, *This is the way we walk to school, walk to school, walk to school. This is the way we walk to school, so early in the morning.* At the same time, their plump teacher stood next to the record player, her eyes on the children, watching; her hand hovering above the spinning record, waiting. Then just when the four-year-olds settled into a rhythm, she touched the tonearm. The small needle skittered across the record and the music stopped. Chairs bumped and screeched as children scurried to secure a seat. With each passing round, one more child would fall away. The first out was often the kid who seemed to have a wandering mind; next to go was the one with the tiny powerless elbows who kept getting pushed aside. The music resumed, until in the end, one child—luckier or stronger or faster than the rest— plunked down in the last remaining chair. This was the first game I learned. It was taught to me once and again inside school and out. As I would later realize, there weren't enough chairs in life for all of us.

Fizz and I watched through the door with a particular memory because it was musical chairs that first brought us together. I had been skipping along, pretending to drag a comb through my hair, singing, *This is the way we comb our hair*, and while working out the last of my imaginary tangles, I noticed Fizz's honey-colored eyes peering at me. At that moment in the song, Fizz leaned over and whispered in a ploy to distract me, "My hair's longer than yours."

"No it's not," I said, irritated by such an obvious remark. All children, like the adults around us, were as conscious of hair length and texture as we were of skin color. That is to say, long hair and light skin gave a child merit just as good hygiene, finished homework, and good home training did. These things suggested you were a child of standing or at least some potential, until proven otherwise. It was a foregone conclusion that the thick mane running down Fizz's back was the longest.

"We'll see after school," Fizz threatened. Our rumble ensued. I was the victor until Fizz's backup snuck up on me with a brick in the back of my head. I cried, then Fizz cried. From then on we always played together. Initially, I was drawn to Fizz for the same reason our teachers always stroked her cheeks—her white features fascinated me. Her wispy nose, long eyelashes, and the beauty mark on her left cheek were appreciated all the more because she wasn't high on herself. She could usually be found on the playground covered in grass stains, and when our friend Dwight asked if he could feel her hair, she didn't act stuck-up or mock him. She just lowered her head to his hands.

Dwight was quite taken with Fizz, and so he did what boys are conditioned to do—he tried to conquer her with things, in his case, candy. "Name what you want—Snickers bars, Hershey Kisses, Jolly Rancher sticks?" he prompted us while twisting his nappy hair, which was the dull red of a sucked-over jawbreaker.

Dwight's granddaddy sold candy out of his living room.

Originally the house had been a shotgun. After his wife had two babies, he added an entire new side. Then his daughter grew up, moved out, and came back home with two babies of her own. With no yard left, there was nowhere to build but up, so not only did Dwight have unlimited access to candy, he had the only two-story house in the 'hood, with a staircase we all longed to climb, but no one more than Teresa. She lived near Dwight in a four-room house the size of a car shed. The only person with a house smaller than hers was Jason Jackson, who was always begging for candy, pencils, and nickels for extra milk.

Later on it became clear to me that even if we employed the same skills that were required to win at musical chairs— intuition, flexibility, and a great deal of stamina—the winner, no, the survivor, would still be determined by a lucky spin of the chair. Never would there be enough seats for all five of us.

I remember once, during recess, Fizz, Dwight, Teresa, Jason, and I sat in a circle cross-legged as if surrounding a campfire.

"What would you do if you could do anything?" Dwight mused conspiratorially.

Teresa smiled demurely, her lips shining like black patent leather. "I'd marry you," she replied, only half joking. At the time that seemed unlikely, since Dwight wanted to run away and be a bass player in a group like the Jackson Five. Fizz just smiled at him, dumbfounded. Jason stared out. This was around the time he stopped allowing himself to smile. For practical reasons, he was becoming distant—at his house, there was no telephone for him to call us, and he knew our mothers forbade us to visit his home because of its filthiness.

"Come on, Jason," I coaxed, tickling his ear with a blade of grass.

"Shut up talking to me, Yolanda," he warned, slapping my hand.

When we first met in preschool, I had shared Jason's anger. Instead of slapping hands, I would pinch the girls at nap time, the way I'd seen Jack pinch Momma, but my need to torture others disappeared once Jack left. With nothing under his control, Jason's rage only grew. Since he couldn't wield power through candy, he mastered another technique that little boys learn—intimidation.

Jason started to hurt us with his hands and bitter words. That way he'd be sure that no one would tease him—not for the one shirt he had to wear several times a week, the dried snot that collected under his nose, or the lopsided bush that grew uncontrollably from his head.

"Kee, kee, kee," he'd utter with a grin after spewing a spitball on the back of someone's neck. It was no surprise then that he missed a great opportunity the day the white lady bounced into our classroom like Raggedy Ann, a violin in her hand.

"Now class," she said to us in a froggy voice, "you are going to hear two sounds, one right after the other. If the second sound is higher than the first, mark answer A. If the second sound is lower than the first, mark your answer B. If the second sound is the same as the first, mark your answer C."

Jason was, as usual, late for school, so he didn't get all the instructions. The next week Miss Jordan came back and called out the names of the three children who'd been selected to play the violin, cello, and viola. Jason Jackson, the one who was always playing the drums on top of his desk and could imitate perfectly a ballad or a groove, was not one of them. Dwight, Teresa, and I made up the list and followed behind the gangly woman, singing, *This is the way we play the strings, play the strings, play the strings. This is the way we play the strings, so early in the morning.*

My getting selected for orchestra class was a fluke. I'm practically tone deaf. Nevertheless, Momma kept applauding my screeching interpretation of "Twinkle, Twinkle, Little Star." Now Teresa's viola made a sweet sound from the very first time she pressed her chin against its wood and drew her bow across the strings, but with a new baby at home, there was nowhere for her to practice, so "Twinkle" was the only song she ever learned. I understood her leaving because I had gone home with her and seen her bent over the kitchen sink, a pile of dirty dishes blocking the water spout. The rest of the house was just as disheveled—worn-out carpet, cracked windowpanes, doors that didn't close properly. The only luxuries contained in the house were the piles of expensive clothes Teresa's mother bought with her salesclerk discount and a console television set. With three little brothers sleeping in a bed next to hers, solitude came only when she pulled the sheets over her head at night.

I, too, would have abandoned my instrument eventually, if it hadn't been for that feeling I got the night the youth orchestra performed with the Shreveport Symphony. In my cancan skirt, I felt special, set apart, and looked over at Dwight in his clip-on tie, thinking he felt the same. Instead he felt ostracized and alone.

Jason seized on the opportunity to reclaim his friend like a dog takes to a squirrel. He'd tease Dwight mercilessly every time he caught him carrying his cello. Dwight was so tormented he took to eating his pencil lead, which he needed the day our third-grade class took our achievement test. When the little booklets were handed out, Fizz laid her head on her desk, complaining of a headache. A few years later when she got thick glasses, I wondered if she had needed them all along.

Because of her pretty dresses and neat penmanship, Teresa had been Miss Margery's favorite student. "Young people," she would declare, holding up Teresa's paper, "this is how a completed work product should look." Teresa would smile quietly, swinging her feet in Yo-Yo sandals underneath her desk. But when our scores determined that I had a quicker mind than Teresa's tidy one, Miss Margery began to encourage me to hold my hand up high. At the same time, when Fizz whispered with her would-be suitors or applied lip gloss in class, our teacher turned a blind eye. All we knew to be was what others expected. So while Teresa and I competed for the best answers, Fizz tossed back her hair, laughing.

That strange year of changes and separations would end with me in the hospital, of all places. A knot the size of a Blow Pop had grown from my wrist, and the doctor said it had to be removed. The tumor was benign, so the thing I thought would doom me turned out to be a saving grace in the end. While I was confined to the hospital's four stark walls with no cable TV to distract me, I read *Are You There God? It's Me, Margaret, Fat Summer,* and a Hardy Boys mystery. I finished them during the first day, and Momma brought me more. The books made me feel like I had a life inside a life. Even when I wasn't reading, I was daydreaming about the characters in the books, empathizing with poor Margaret and thrilled about all the weight the fat boy lost during a summer job mowing lawns. The stories took me somewhere else and gave me a whole new set of friends.

When I returned to school, Fizz and Teresa shared inside jokes, Dwight and Jason squatted in front of the chalkboard serving out a punishment, while I was made to spend recess in the library until my stitches healed. I came to anticipate those strolls to the library, the brightest room in the school. Enormous fluorescent beams held spotlights on all my new friends— Huck Finn, Harriet the Spy, and the wonderful pig Wilbur.

"Good morning, Miss Yolanda," Mrs. Jefferson greeted me, then added, while patting down her burgundy 'fro, "So who will it be today, Judy Blume or Nancy Drew?"

In the privacy of my mind, I was inspired to begin forming some pretty grand plans for my future: I'd go to some fancy college far away from home, where in winter there would be snow on the ground; after that maybe I would become a lawyer or even a judge. Sometimes, when I was really smelling myself, I'd fancy myself a writer spending my afternoons with characters like those I visited in books. My dreams were gratifying until I tried to picture Fizz and the others with me. When I couldn't, I'd get a little sad and lonely and try to slow myself down again.

I figured, once I got where I was going, people would be curious about how I came to be there at all and want to know what happened to everybody else. I would tell them about my early dreams, share loving stories about my childhood friends, and assure my listeners that I was not exceptional among my schoolmates. (I'd linger here, long enough for them to feel the weight of my words.) Then I'd share the sad revelation that my story makes clear—not every child is given the same chance.

My observers, especially those not acquainted with the place where I come from, would want me to explain this further. To get it through their heads, I'd have to make a full circle like a needle spinning on a vinyl record and begin by explaining that in Head Start there was a game we played called musical chairs.

Tornadoes

Who has gathered the wind in the hollow
of his hand? Tell me if you know.

—*Proverbs 30:4*

Excepting the winter months, when it was a bit chilly, the temperature in Shreveport seldom dipped below seventy degrees F,
so ice cream trucks jingled through our neighborhoods most of
the year. Our driver, Mr. Crouch, was a white man with gray
whiskers that stuck from his chin like stickpins from a sewing
cushion. Knowing my love for sherbet push-ups, he would pass
my block most evenings. I would usually beg around until I had
collected enough change for my treat, but the day after a hand-
ful of tiny whirlwinds danced across the city, Pappy suggested
I work for my money.

"Look around," he said, pointing out the scattered garbage
and cans strewn in the street. "Don't you see where the tornado
winds have left you opportunity?"

Dragging a large trash bag behind me, I set out collecting

bottles and cans to sell for recycling. It wasn't long before I needed a break. Spotting Honeymoon's neighbor sitting on a rusted metal chair in front of her house, I stopped there. Mrs. Leviston was the oldest lady in the neighborhood, funny-looking in an infirm sort of way. She seldom wore her teeth but was never without her glasses, which made her eyes bug as if they were about to spring into her lap. Behind her, staring at me through a window, were the eyes of antique dolls. She had all kinds—white, black, even some "orientals." "The worst thing a person can be," I remember her saying one day, her cane leaning idly at her knee, "is discriminatory." She was often parceling out such words of discernment.

"What you doing in that street, girl?" Mrs. Leviston called out to me.

"Collecting cans. You got any?"

"I might, but you need to come out of that street. Tornado's coming back again."

"You think so?" I asked, looking up just then at the odd rainbow of gray hues covering the sky. It was obvious that the stillness had alerted her.

Tornadoes whirled in the spring mostly, but sometimes it seemed as if they happened regardless of the season. Summer had just turned to fall that year, yet they came one after the other. Most of us hadn't ever even seen a really powerful one. Children were usually huddled inside a bathtub when they ripped through. But afterward we could see their footprints: the upturned oak tree lying in the street, its roots already beginning to rot; brick debris scattered like pebbles in the road; and streetlights bowing to a greater power.

Sometimes tornadoes approached while we were in school, so teachers oversaw warning drills to make sure we were prepared. If the bell sounded off in one unbroken clang, we knew it was the real thing. Otherwise, three high-pitched rings followed by commands from our teacher Mr. Morton signaled it was time to duck under our desks for another exercise.

To make us understand the seriousness of such practice, Mr. Morton explained, "What's so particular about tornadoes is that they hit in the same place time after time. Then, when you least expect it, *wham!*" he'd say, slamming his hand on a desktop. "A ceiling falls in on your head."

Mrs. Leviston was right—the thermal instability, the thick, humid air, the still silence that suggested "the quiet before the storm"—all were signs that a tornado was coming. This frightened me, but Mrs. Leviston seemed as calm as a worm in mud.

"Come up here and sit with me awhile," she invited. "I'll see what I have in the kitchen a little later."

I climbed the concrete stairs to her and sat down.

"You ever get tired of just sitting up here all day, Mrs. Leviston?"

"Child, please," she said, a mist of tobacco sap punctuating the remark. Taking another pinch of the snuff from the pack on her apron pocket she added, "I'm not just sitting. I'm watching and thinking."

" 'Bout what?" I asked, watching her squirt black juice from her mouth into a Folgers coffee can.

"I'm old, girl," she said, sucking her gums. "I got a lot to think about."

I looked up at Mrs. Leviston. Her curved back was propped up against a pillow. Loose skin hung from her thighs, then swelled around her ankles and feet. The face sagged like a deflated balloon. Before I could stop the words from coming out, I asked her age.

She winked at me and said, "Alls I can tell you is that I'm closer to a hundred than I am eighty-five."

"You must know everything," I said in amazement.

"No, baby. One thing I know for sure is that you can never know everything. Just like you can never know people."

"What do you mean by that?" I asked, kicking a fly off my leg.

"I mean you never know what people are capable of. How one you might think is a good person will lie until they turn cold. While someone you despise and know ain't worth a dime might one day up and do the right thing. I tell you. I gave up being surprised at things for my eightieth birthday."

"Why then?" I asked.

"I figured I was getting too old to be shocked. I might give myself a heart attack." We both laughed, but Mrs. Leviston's tone became serious. "Sometimes we think people are good who turn out to be bad. Sometimes an evil coon can redeem himself. Sometimes we never know, like we won't ever know about that gray boy who tried to make himself at home here."

She was referring to Mr. Morton, our tornado drill instructor at school. Mrs. Leviston saw him weaving in and out of our streets, sunning by the little bayou behind our school, teasing the children as he drove by. Because he was our only white teacher, he stuck out like a stick of chalk in a Crayola box, but was useful enough. He seemed old to me at the time, but actually he must have been fairly young—almost thirty or so. His skin was pig pink, his hair red, and his mustache a color in between. Although his face carried a drab expression and his tone was serious, as a teacher he was playful. When it was his day to be in charge of recess, he didn't stand in the shade with a yardstick the way the other teachers did. He would march flat-footed onto the field with his hairy ankles sticking out of his leather basketball shoes and play dodgeball with the boys, trying to hit them as hard as he could. The girls in their ribbons and plaid dresses would circle him and fight to hold his hand. I didn't like holding Mr. Morton's hand, and I told him so one day.

"Why is that, Yolanda?" he asked.

"Because your hands are sweaty and they smell funny." Then considering this I asked, "Do we smell funny to you?"

"Just your hair," he offered with a bemused grin.

"That's just the boys' Mr. Puff soft spray and the girls' Oil Sheen," I explained.

Our familiarity stemmed from the time he spent as my fourth-grade basketball coach. I was a lazy, sluggish player, but the tallest on the team. Quite naturally Mr. Morton stayed on my back. "Yolanda, get your big butt back down that court. How could you let that little girl take that ball from you?" The best part about being on the team was the ride to and from our games in the back of Mr. Morton's red pickup. He didn't get nervous when we stood up in back or tussled over who would hold the basketballs. Sometimes the games weren't over until well after dark. Each girl would beg to be the last one dropped off at home.

Our game travel arrangements didn't raise any eyebrows until one spring day during morning recess, a knock-kneed girl named Roni confided that Mr. Morton had touched her the night before. The basketball girls snorted in disbelief, as if we'd been told of a Bigfoot sighting. Then the reality of it began to unfold. The custodian escorted Mr. Morton from his classroom. Within the hour Roni's father arrived pointing the barrel of his shotgun. And our basketball season ended.

In different ways Mr. Morton and Roni were both persecuted.

My opinion kept shifting in the wind. First I searched my mind for ways to blame Mr. Morton. Then, feeling guilty, I'd think about Mr. Morton's patience with me and how he'd been so generous with his time. Time that some of our parents didn't give us.

Our science textbooks said that tornadoes were formed when a mass of hot air collides with a swell of cold. At Mr. Morton's trial, the hot-headed black parents collided with dismissive administrators to produce the same effect. The children were left out like shocked birds whose wings had been wrenched away in a violent wind. It had never occurred to us to mistrust a teacher and certainly not one who took such care with us.

"So do you think Mr. Morton messed with that girl?" I asked Mrs. Leviston, as if she could know for sure. She just puckered her lips as if exaggerating a kiss and tossed a clump of what looked to be black jelly into her can. "You'd know better than me. Did he ever touch you or look at you funny?" she asked.

"Never," I said emphatically.

"Well," she said, looking at me over her glasses, "it sounds like you know in your gut what happened."

The trial was all the folks in Stoner Hill talked about that summer. In the barbershop, church halls, and back-alley juke joints, the question was the same: "What happened between that white man and that little black girl?"

The night before jury selection, Momma opened her front door to find portly Mrs. Davis pleading Mr. Morton's case. When she held out a clipboard holding several pages of an unsigned petition, Momma asked what I thought was a pretty good question, "How can you petition for Mr. Morton's innocence when we haven't heard the facts?" Its soundness was lost on the other woman.

"You listen here," Mrs. Davis said through tight lips, pointing her finger. "That man has worked with all my children, never raising a finger to hurt them."

Mrs. Davis's passion prompted Momma to show her the door. Many people tried not to take sides, but others joined in the standoff. On one side were the superstitious, who relied on root spells, cod liver oil, and daily church visits to save their children. Then there were the peace breakers and ranting lunatics who couldn't pass you in a grocery-store aisle or let you sit peacefully in a beautician's chair without offering a warning of the sinister deeds being plotted against us, Mr. Morton's being one.

Mr. Morton had stopped driving his red truck around the neighborhood long before the courts found him not guilty. Still, with another basketball season beginning I yearned for the truth.

As though reading my mind, Mrs. Leviston assured me, "Girl, you ain't got to know that. Some things just between a man and his God." I still wondered if maybe Mr. Morton was getting away with something. But Mrs. Leviston leaned over toward me, wiping her hands on her apron. "Girl," she said, "I done lived long enough to know don't nobody get away with nothing. You hear me?"

A tornado did touch down in the city that day, but not in our neighborhood. It struck across the river in Bossier City. Metal rooftops ripped away and flew through the air like sheets of paper torn from a notebook. In a moment, a row of dainty white houses were shredded down to the level of the picket fences that surrounded them. The next day Momma and I drove through the town and saw apartments cracked open like dollhouses, cement spread along the street like crumbs swept off a lap, and trailer homes with sucked-in jaws. Three people died, more than two hundred were injured, and two thousand were left homeless.

It's hard to fathom a neighborhood ripping open in a single moment, but that year two did. It seemed that nothing would ever be the same—and nothing was. After the neighbors and firemen cleared the debris and the search for survivors ended, the families began to rebuild—plank by plank, nail by nail. Some worked harder than others to get their houses back up. And so it was with the aftermath of our scandal in Stoner Hill—there were those who continued to point a finger and circulate feelings of distrust. But I listened to Mrs. Leviston and accepted that I would never know what happened or why, that all I could do was try and rebuild trust in the people around me.

The teachers came out of the shade and joined the children at recess, and a balding black teacher took over our basketball program. Like those building new houses after the tornado, our school took great care to ensure that our foundation was more solid than it had been before. It was as if the disaster had somehow given the town a will to build things better. The tornado had come in and pruned the community. We would grow back fuller and stronger than we had been. Even Roni, who never spoke to us about what happened, could be seen above the crowd, smiling atop the monkey bars. In order to fortify myself with Mrs. Leviston's insight, I climbed the steps that led up to her front porch often in the years that followed and hoped that, like her, I'd be able to stand firm whenever rough winds blew.

The Long Walk to Honeymoon's

You are old, and your children do not walk in your ways.

—I Samuel 8:4

During my elementary-school years, I must have made the walk to Honeymoon's house at least five thousand times. It was hardly more than a block from any of the places to which I generally traveled, and I instinctively knew the way. Sometimes Momma sent me there on an errand, perhaps to borrow a large pot; sometimes I went of my own volition to indulge in a bowl of Honeymoon's chicken and dumplings or to listen with Pappy to a baseball radio broadcast. Down our long driveway I would shuffle in my white Converse tennis shoes. Then I'd wobble alongside the cement gutters anchoring the street. At the peak of the hill, I would turn right and skip the half block to Honeymoon's door.

I frequently strolled to Honeymoon's from church. Because of the four-lane highway that split the street that both Honeymoon and St. Peter Baptist shared, this journey was laced with a level of danger thrilling to a little girl.

Most often I'd trek from Stoner Hill Elementary School. Two distinct paths led from there to Honeymoon's house. I could dart down the school's sloping playground, toppling the bucket-high ant beds that cluttered my way, and scamper to Honeymoon's in less time than it took me to spell M-I-S-S-I-S-S-I-P-P-I. On the occasions when I knew that Honeymoon wouldn't be home yet and there'd be no hot-water corn bread waiting for me, I would lollygag, venturing down the back of the school's narrow, rocky dead-end back street that sprang from a graveyard and was named Hopewell. Many times I'd passed its slouching, broken-down houses, my nose and throat filling with the taste of tobacco before the irony of the street's name ever occurred to me. Once I reached Honeymoon's, rushing through the screen door was like pulling open the hatch to a sweet, toasty oven. I'd sit at her wobbly kitchen table eating corn bread so sweet it tasted like cake. Honeymoon, busy picking red peppers and stuffing them into the pockets of her crawfish-print apron, would see me from the backyard and raise her plum-tomato cheeks in my direction, saying, "Hi, Londa. I been waiting on you, dear."

One chilly morning in January, I was rushed off to Honeymoon's so fast that I left my new velour sweater hanging from the back of my chair at school. Children were still in morning classes, and grown-ups were all at work, so I slowed myself as soon as I was alone on the hushed streets. I was careful not to walk on any cracks in the sidewalk; if I misstepped, I took twenty paces back, then started over again. I took time to notice Mr. Horn's old Plymouth stretching out morosely atop bricks in the middle of his front yard and to bury my face in the honeysuckle that had exploded onto the sidewalk.

That day's walk had begun not on the back street or on the playground but in the principal's office. Our fifth-grade class had returned from Christmas vacation, and we were busy flaunting our bounty. Dwight was showing off his double belt, a leather strap that wrapped twice around his waist. Teresa played with the new decorative combs in her hair, and Fizz wore magical soft suede shoes with clear soles.

As was often the case, Jason had returned to school empty-handed. Having nothing to display but his temperament, he kept poking his fingers into my arms, but I wouldn't turn away from my new vocabulary book. Peering over my shoulder, Jason watched me insert the missing words into the essay titled "Playground Thrill." The sentence was "The ————— grabbed the ————— on the ————— and rode until he got dizzy." I was to choose from the words "Dick", "merry-go-round," "balls," "cat," "monkey bars," "student," "handles," and "jump rope." I was about to select the appropriate words when Jason's hand grabbed my pencil and lightly wrote, in order, "cat," "balls," and "Dick." "Go ahead," he said grinning, "it'll be funny." I stared back at Jason nervously and shook my head no. "Scaredy-cat, scaredy-balls, scaredy-drawers," he mouthed the last word. I wasn't afraid of Jason, but I also didn't like his teasing, so I darkly scribbled in the words in time for Mrs. Prigg to walk by and catch me.

"Yolanda, come with me," she commanded as soon as her eye caught my page. I followed her clanking heels down the outside corridor to a seat on the stiff vinyl sofa in the principal's office. I watched her go behind the half counter that separated the children from the officials and pull out my file. The receptionist peered at me accusingly while Mrs. Prigg talked to my mother on the phone.

"Mrs. Smith," she said casually, rubbing the mole that sat on the side of her nose like a misplaced black bean, "I'd like to read you something Yolanda wrote in class today. 'The cat grabbed the balls on the Dick and rode until she got dizzy.' " After a long pause with the receiver still at her ear she said to Momma, "I know, I know. I never had any trouble like this from you." Then after another pause, "It's too bad you're at work, or I'd send her right home." And the final one, "Oh really? That's what she needs. Yes, yes, I'll do just that."

After replacing the receiver, Mrs. Prigg leaned over the counter, allowing the heating vent to fan her hair, and motioned with her long fingernails for me to come near. She bent down further so that we were eye to eye and in a deceptively calm voice instructed me, "You are to walk to your grandmother's house, get your whipping, and march right back to school. Do you understand?"

"Yes, ma'am," I said, liquid flooding my eyes and mouth.

Maybe I'll be lucky enough to just get the belt, I thought to myself along the way. No, the belt was reserved for simple offenses like Ruby and I getting into a fight at the dinner table. For something like this I might have to pick my own switch or worse—get the extension cord. This was the last time I was going to act without thinking, I said to myself. A person could stand only so many beatings.

When Honeymoon heard the clank of the fence outside, she slowly opened the front door with a warm greeting. "Come on in, Londa. I been waitin' on you." She stood in the doorway of her bedroom. She had a serious yet slightly bemused look on her face. Her hands were on her hips, and she seemed to be out of breath.

"It took me a minute to find my strap," she said, waving the thin cord in my direction. Before she began to whip me, she sat on the edge of her bed folding her cotton skirt between her legs. I tried explaining to Honeymoon how I'd been tricked into writing in that book and how the other kids were always saying stuff that was much worse than that.

Honeymoon looked at me and shook her head. "Londa, sit down for a minute. I'm gon' tell you something." I gratefully obliged. "You ain't got the luxury of doing what everybody else does," she said to me in a sad tone. "I know what you did is nothing compared to what some of my white folks' children get away with all the time, and you should hear the way some of the little ones talk to the ones who birthed 'em. Lordy be," she said, throwing her eyes to the back of her head. "Some of them children ain't got no manners and no respect for adults, but they white and they got money, so they gon' always have opportunities. You black and poor, so you gon' always need people to help you. But people don't help sassy, filthy-mouth girls. You understand me?"

Unaccustomed to much talking prior to a lashing, I had not intended to take anything from what Honeymoon said, but her words struck me as untrue, so I said to her, "We not poor, Honeymoon. The kids who live on the edge of the Hill and have free lunch tickets are poor." I was referring to the Stoner Vista projects that were stacked on one another like crumbled matchboxes, but Honeymoon said those people were beyond poor, they were pitiful.

"See," she continued, "people look out for children who are polite and say, 'Yes, ma'am' and don't give them any trouble. That's the kind of girl you better be from now on." Then standing up she said to me, "Now, Londa, my back went out on me this morning, so I can't chase you around this house. You got to stand here and take your whipping. Do you understand?"

"Honeymoon," I said pleadingly, "if you don't feel good, you don't have to whip me. I promise I understand."

"No, Londa. I got to whip you, so I can make sure the stinging stays in your head. I ain't gon' always have time to explain to you why this is right and that is wrong. I got to make it so you gon' do right automatically 'cause you remember what it feels like when you do wrong."

With those words, she lifted the tight wire strap, and using all the strength in her arm without extending her back, she flung the cord against my legs. I immediately screamed and fell to the floor kicking. After a few moments the sting subsided and Honeymoon hit me again . . . and again. Before long, I was on my way back to school, legs smarting with every step. I passed the same things—the tiny shacks with missing roof shingles, the wrecked cars that crowded dirt front yards, the weed-filled lawns that grew out of control—but it was as if I was seeing them for the first time, and I realized what it meant to be poor.

Contrary to what Honeymoon had said, this revelation was in no way associated with the beating she'd just inflicted on me. It was the other thing that she'd done that was a break from the spanking routine. She had taken the time to talk to me, to explain the consequences of what I had done wrong. I was certain that it was the explaining that had made the difference, because I'd felt the sting of dry leather against wet skin just a week earlier at Big Momma's house. I didn't realize it at the time, but that one too had to do with us being poor.

It was over the Christmas break, and Big Momma was hiding out from her insurance agent because she wouldn't have the $11.43 to pay him until her Social Security check arrived. Every day the white gentleman knocked on the door and Big Momma and I sat listening behind drawn curtains. I wasn't fully grasping why we were doing this, but I was certainly old enough to know it wasn't just a game. Nevertheless, when Big Momma was finally able to open the curtains and greet the man with his check, I ruined the moment by embarrassing her.

"I came by yesterday, Miz Frazier, but no one was here," the man insisted, puzzled.

"Oh, I hate I missed you," Big Momma said, her face slightly contorting from the stress of the lie. Before she could get him out the door, I blurted out, "We were here. We were just hiding from you."

Seeing Big Momma's fawn skin turn as red as Honeymoon's tomatoes, I was overcome with nervous laughter. After uttering some fragmented words, Big Momma closed the door and just looked at me. It was as though the anger and shame mixed in a way that made her speechless. She just stomped away. We ate in silence, and then Big Momma prepared for our baths.

She didn't fill the tub with water and dishwashing liquid the way Momma did at home. She ran just three inches of water, and we had to share it. Big Momma always went first and afterward would call me in to clean in the dirty water. The only thing left to split would have been the air. That's how poor Big Momma was, but she didn't know how to tell me that, so she slapped my fanny instead. She pulled my wet body out of that tub and stung me with a leather belt. I screamed with surprise and pain as water splashed on her thinly painted white walls. All Big Momma could bring herself to say with her tongue stuck in the bottom of her lip was, "Don' ever embarrass me like da' again."

I didn't remember the whippings themselves, only the humiliation that accompanied them. Having to hear them say, "I didn't raise you like that." If I wrapped all my whippings together, they'd be as light as a ball of rubber bands, but Honeymoon's words—that we were poor, that I was a disappointment, that I had shamed my family—hung from my neck with the weight of a cotton gin.

I was only ten at the time, but even then I realized that to fulfill my grandmother's request, I would have to separate the lessons she attempted to teach me from the methods she employed, the way a farmer separates the wheat from the chaff. I determined to diverge from her path, take detours and some shortcuts. Only from a different road could I look back one day and appreciate that those streets I'd trailed to Honeymoon's held hope after all.

Take Me Now, Lord, Take Me Now

> She is a tree of life to those who embrace her; those who
> lay hold of her will be blessed.
>
> —*Proverbs 3:18*

Riding through the neighborhood where Honeymoon worked, I once remarked to Momma that the yards seemed to mirror the lives of its residents. Here the yards were divided into neat squares of dark green. Long strands of monkey grass draped their flower beds, matching bushes dotted the door frames, and a lush magnolia tree stood in the middle of most yards. These people led ordered lives.

Our neighborhood wasn't like that. With no fancy grass or sidewalks to divide them, the yards seemed to curl into one another and it seemed that every tree God created found a home somewhere around there. At Honeymoon's alone there were fig, pecan, and pear trees as well as several willows. During ripe months, the nectar from lemons and sassafras scented the streets. A few houses down from Momma's, a family cleared eleven trees from a lot, leaving only a perfectly round one with drooping branches of creamy white flowers to shade a new trailer home. There was an oak, left barren and charred after a house fire, that became the epitome of ugliness: "You look as sorry as that oak on the corner of Stoner," we'd say to one another. The rows of oaks duplicated along the highway were worse than ugly—they were ordinary. I hardly noticed them at all, and when I did it was only to wonder how they had come to be so boring. Was it a lack of water or sunlight that kept their leaves thin and faint in color, or were they simply at the mercy of their father? After all, no matter how much you water it, an oak will never grow into a pine.

I was fascinated by the trees, especially the way they grew— an army of little sprouts fastening around a much larger chief root charging straight into the ground. Girls grow a lot like that, our interests first shooting off in a dozen different directions until the essence of our nature takes hold. Early on, with all my uncles surrounding me, my disposition was more like a boy's. I cared how high I could jump, how far I could stretch my limbs. After Jason Jackson, I was the best fistfighter in my class. Then, seemingly just one day, these two lumps popped out of my chest, changing everything. I used to love wearing halter tops, but I stopped the day my uncle Michael joked in front of everybody, "Look at those buds Yolanda's growing!" Momma admonished him for making me self-conscious, but the damage had been done. From that day, no matter how hot it got, I covered myself with a blue-jean jacket.

Others unintentionally belittled me as well. There was the church lady who interrupted my self-loathing to thumb her nose at me in disapproval. "You walk like you're stepping over cow droppings, and why do you dress like a tomboy?" Another tapped into my greatest fear by teasing that I looked and acted like my father. The few things that I did still like about myself—my height, my eyes, the length of my hair—were things that I'd inherited from Jack. What if I also shared his penchant for liquor and would eventually waste my life away? As I struggled to figure this all out, my family formed camps around me.

Baby Jane had thought that since I was tall and watched sports incessantly, I should focus on my basketball. Unfortunately, we discovered that height and enthusiasm were no match for my opponents' agility and natural coordination. But Baby Jane didn't give up easily, and every October he would take me to Lorant's Sporting Goods Store and buy me jogging shorts, T-shirts, wristbands, and a pair of white high-top Converse basketball shoes, like the ones Dr. J wore, and on Sunday afternoons we'd walk over to the courts behind Stoner Hill.

As I ran layups and shot free throws, Baby Jane's expression changed like the clouds casting shadows behind him. When I made three baskets in a row, he'd grin like a horse and say something like, "Life is about mastering the fundamentals. Once you've got 'em down, no one can shake your confidence." On the more frequent occasions when I lost control of the ball or just stopped trying altogether, Baby Jane would wipe the sweat building beneath his plastic visor and pull his lips back in a snarl of gold-capped teeth. When I asked a question he'd already answered several times, he'd give me the Tin Man's blank gaze. Before any practice ended, I had usually seen each of his reflections of pride, disgust, and dismay.

On my return home after one particularly grueling practice, Momma was not at all pleased to see my face stained with sweat and dirt and my hair springing messily all over my head.

She grabbed me by the arm and commanded, "Start acting like a young lady."

"Why do you say that?" I asked, incensed more by her words than by her grip. Momma's response was to enroll me in the Alpha Kappa Alpha–sponsored charm school one of her co-workers had invited me to. For the next six weeks I missed my Saturday-morning TV lineup of *Fat Albert, Oh, Mighty Isis,* and *Electra Woman and Dyna Girl* in order to sit in a meeting hall, stuffed in taffeta dresses and thick old-lady stockings, along with nineteen other sixth-grade "charmers," and be educated on womanly virtues by a swarm of rouge-cheeked women in pink. I walked with a book on my head and was drilled in the fine art of sitting—back straight, legs crossed at the ankle, never at the knee, with feet slightly tilted to one side. I learned how to drink tea from china cups, at which time I pointed out that I never drank tea.

"Mmm, thank you for that observation, Yolanda," came the sorority woman's exasperated reply, cupped in a hollow smile.

I accompanied three other girls, all wearing nail polish and smelling of Tinkerbell perfume, to our "get acquainted" table, where we were instructed to sip tea, make polite conversation, and whatnot. From the conversation, I gathered my fellow charmers all knew one another. They lived on the same cul-de-sac in Twilight Meadows—one of those uppity black neighborhoods that mimicked the white folks' neatly trimmed lawns. Since they all attended the same newly built church and air-conditioned school, all eyes fell on me. "Is your momma a teacher too?" a cute chimp-faced girl asked.

"No, she's an operator for the telephone company," I offered civilly enough.

Another, wearing diamond earrings, introduced herself as

Tiffany and asked, "What about your daddy? What does he do?" The question slammed me like a brick upside my head. No one had ever asked me about him before. All my friends just seemed to know why Jack was no longer around. Ordinarily, I would have kicked in with a wry answer like "For all I know, still hiding under Mr. Jim's porch," or taken my questioner into a headlock, but neither fallback was appropriate at a lace-covered card table set with linen napkins and porcelain plates and surrounded by prissy little girls.

I managed a muffled "He's not around." The girls moved on to another topic of conversation, politely leaving me alone with the pain of my thoughts and the sting of shame. Before long one of our AKA hosts was walking around inspecting us and explaining what it was to be a lady.

"It is always an honor to be thought of as a lady, and it is a job that never ends," she said, lightly tapping elbows and requesting their removal from tables. "Ladies don't raise their voices to shout something across the room or, God forbid, into another room." She stopped then and looked around at us, and in a whisper that presumed a secret she continued, "A lady always waits for the gentleman to pull out her chair or open the door. If a young man does not do these things, then a lady knows that he is not the man for her. Ladies are always well groomed," she went on, holding out her pink nails, "with clean, buffed nails and neat hair."

It took the ladies of Alpha Kappa Alpha about three weeks to get me to buy into this, but after that I was exhibiting decidedly better posture and planning what I wanted to wear for the Charmers Fashion Show Finale. Each girl needed six outfits, crisp, colorful, and preferably new. Momma was strapped for cash, so she charged my clothes but offered a disclaimer to the

Palais Royal Department Store saleslady. "That daughter of mine grows so fast, I'm not even sure if these will fit." This way she would have an excuse when, after I modeled the dresses and jumpsuits, she returned them to the store.

For the event Momma hot-pressed my hair and flipped it back like Farrah Fawcett's on *Charlie's Angels.*

"You look pretty good," Michael said, and the smiles on Momma and Honeymoon lit the room. "Oh," Big Momma purred, "what a lady you're turning out to be."

And that sports thing? Around that time I stopped watching Dick Cavett's HBO sports show in favor of listening to Ruby and her friends talk about boys. I carried a purse, the contents of which included a comb, a brush, and a stick of cherry Tinkerbell lip gloss as well as my little plastic-covered napkins. I got tired of Baby Jane yelling at me when I tried not to mess up my hair, so I quit basketball and convinced Momma I could be like the other charmers if I got a perm.

The following week we drove to the spot between Church's Fried Chicken and Booker T. Washington High School, where sat Claire's Beauty Shop, a dingy room off of the owner's kitchen. Stapled to Claire's greasy walls were glossy pictures of black women torn from advertisements in *Ebony* magazine. While parting my hair, Claire swore that she could make me look like any one of those models using a procedure she called a "press-'n'-perm."

With Momma's blessing, Claire began applying a white cream that smelled like ammonia all over my hair. With each cold brush of lye, my scalp tingled and my eyes teared. On Claire's radio, Rose Royce fittingly bellowed, "I'm going down."

"Is it burning?" Claire asked in a hoarse voice over her shoulder.

"Yeeesssss!" I screamed out in pain. She quickly rinsed my hair, then forgot me under a hot dryer for over an hour. When I was seated back in her chair, iron combs from a hot plate resembling a butter dish were raked through my hair. When the heat and hair grease met, my scalp sizzled and steam rose. A few times a hot piece of hair burnt my neck. Though the process was painful, I found the result—straight and shiny hair—well worth it.

It was January by then, and Momma agreed that I could begin the year by managing my own hair. I experimented with styles. My favorite was a braid down one side with floppy curls hanging from the other. Quite a bit of hair came out every time I combed it. Claire saw large patches of it wash down her sink. While Momma administered the evil eye, Claire tried an assortment of "deep conditioners," "hair reconstructors," and "hot oil treatments" to save my tresses, but nothing worked.

My mane shed for the rest of the school year. Standing in the processional line at my sixth-grade graduation, I looked as if I were wearing a bird's nest on top of my head. Jason Jackson stood behind me teasing.

There was a popular television show at the time called *Sanford and Son*. The lead character was a widower named Fred, and his nemesis was his sister-in-law, Esther. She was a tall woman with manly features, swollen eyes, a big face, and a slight overbite. Whenever she harassed Fred or he simply felt like offending her, he'd grab his chest with one hand and throw the other up to the sky, backing up as if he were having a heart attack and yelling, "Take me now, Lord, take me now."

Jason said he couldn't decide which was uglier—that burnt-oak, bug-eyed Esther, or me. Then he grabbed his chest like Sanford and joked, "Take me now, Lord. Take me now." He stopped joking once we entered the auditorium, but I faced further humiliation. I heard Momma saying to Big Momma, "There she is. There's Yolanda."

To which Big Momma replied, "That's Londa? It can't be. Where's her beautiful hair?"

I dropped my head and begged God to take me away from all this.

After the ceremony, I cried to Big Momma that she didn't like me as much without my hair.

"No, baby," she said, "it's not that. I just didn't recognize you is all."

I'd always thought that Big Momma would know me anywhere, even if I wore a sack over my head. But then how could I expect her to know me if I didn't even know myself? Every time I thought I'd grasped hold of the one thing that could give me an identity—basketball, my femininity, my hair—it was snatched away from me, and I was left to wonder if all I'd ever be was a crazy man's daughter. I wished I could fall away from Jack, like a leaf freed by the wind, but I would still have to live with the fact that he was the tree I grew from. I wanted those feelings of inadequacy to go away right then and there, but Big Momma said they'd be with me for a while.

"Time, baby, time. You got lots more growing still to do." Like the trees, I supposed, which grow year after year, ring after ring, greater in beauty. I needed to believe this would also happen to me.

Shallow Water

> The others gathered together and
> stood for their lives, and had rest.
>
> —*Esther 9:16*

For many years St. Peter Baptist Church held its annual Fourth of July picnic at Lake Bistineau. Inhabiting the outer mouth of the creek were schools of shad that gathered in bays and pockets. Hand-size black bream, spotted crappie, and white bass swam up toward the point where the lake drained into the main river channel. Along the water's shelves and ledges, rubber trees swayed in rare breezes above the yellow grass.

In my mind the picnic became the anchor for a full year. "This time last," someone would remark about his recovery from some health malady or financial mishap of some months prior. The refrain could also be a sad reminder of good times gone by or a recently deceased loved one. That was the case for my family the year I slipped from above the water's silver ceiling, falling to its rug of shells and sand, almost drowning.

Momma and I had arrived at Lake Bistineau in the early afternoon. Even though the city was experiencing a drought, it was a humid summer day. The grass, usually a dark silky green, felt like splinters stabbing at my bare feet. Baby Jane and Uncle Wayne were already assembled around one of the barbecue pits, their shoulders slumped, their faces wanting. It was difficult to watch as red veins formed in Momma's eyes and a shallow smile passed her lips, so I turned away and ran toward the water. A gentle wind carried the aroma of burning hickory, cayenne, and beef, and it eddied in the air. Small black grills dotted the picnic area, where women carefully poured brightly colored mustard, relish, and ketchup into bowls. Some of the older kids knotted ropes through eyelets, tying them to poles for a makeshift volleyball net. I walked into the lake staring down at the water sweetly wetting my skin.

I watched the other kids floating around me and tried to relax, even though I couldn't swim. My comfort was short-lived when my legs were knocked from under me. My head hit the bottom. My ears rang out. I opened my eyes and saw wavy legs kicking water into my face.

No one tried to rescue me, not even my friends wading nearby. The water disallowed any cry for help. I could hear muffled laughter but felt no outstretched hand, and in the stilled panic of acceptance that comes when all hope is washed away, I wondered, *Don't they see I'm drowning?*

Earlier that summer Momma's second husband, Calvin, had promised to teach me how to swim. He'd been in my life since he and Momma had met a little over a year earlier at, "of all places," Momma would later say, "a nightclub." The juke joint known as the Hurricane Lounge was a featured attraction in a city with no discos or bars to entertain the young crowd.

Momma shunned the nightlife, but eventually her brothers co-erced her into going with them to collect her own curvacious Hurricane daiquiri glass. Like the first chapter in a book she wished she'd never opened, that night marked a period of abandon for Momma, who found herself married a few months later.

Calvin, by contrast, was a regular at the Hurricane. Like my father, he was tall and had a sad smile. He also liked to drink, only his drinking didn't make him mean. His drinking made him limpsy, mellow, and a great fishing companion. Our fa-vorite thing to do together was throw lines around the cypress on Lake Bistineau. Calvin called it "lazy fishing" because all we'd do was wrap some blood bait—worms or live fish—along limb lines and toss them off a dock into four feet of water. Calvin would whistle softly as we waited for the whiskered fish to sink their cold mouths around death.

Momma knew going in that Calvin liked the bottle. She mar-ried him anyway because he was handsome, docile, and pos-sessed no temper. More important than any of those, he had asked. But by the time my baby brother arrived in late winter, Calvin's Hurricane glasses were crowding the kitchen cabinets and seemed to line all the counters and freestanding shelves. Momma was worried about Calvin's drinking, but since he wasn't uncaring, she was trying to make things work. Unfortu-nately, the "Crown," as he liked to call it, caused his husbandly eyes to wander and his work to suffer.

Momma had confided these concerns to her older brother at the picnic the year before. Uncle Rat understood. He was also in a marriage of struggle, even though you would never have known it to look at the way he and Aunt Shirley had tickled and petted each other in the water while tossing their four children back and forth. Then a few nights after the pit fires had been smothered, about a breath past midnight, a call came from Aunt Shirley. "Come quick," she told Honeymoon. "I just shot Rat."

Honeymoon didn't panic in the moment but moved swiftly, waking Pappy and calling Baby Jane to come. Together they made the hour-and-forty-minute drive to Arkansas in half that time. Aunt Shirley had told them to go to the house, but Honeymoon instructed Pappy to find the hospital. She stormed into the emergency room with Pappy and Baby Jane a few paces behind. At the admitting counter, she inquired about the condition of Uncle Rat. The nurse's green eyes faded, and she asked Honeymoon softly, "Ma'am, who are you?"

"His mother," Honeymoon offered sternly.

The nurse apologized, then told them that Uncle Rat had been dead when they brought him in. Baby Jane dropped to his knees, choking on tears. Pappy stood still, holding his breath. Honeymoon gripped her vinyl purse as if it were a life jacket and demanded to see her son. The nurse walked the heavy threesome down a long corridor, around a quiet corner, and through another set of doors. She and Honeymoon moved quietly in the same white rubber-soled shoes. Pappy and Baby Jane trailed behind in noisy work boots. But nothing was loud enough to disturb Uncle Rat, waiting patiently.

Honeymoon snatched his cover and flung it to the floor, causing a gust of air to flap Pappy's hat. Staring down at Uncle Rat's naked body, Honeymoon cried out, "Lord, have mercy." Then she pointed her index finger toward every gash and puncture she could find. As few mothers could, she observed three punctures, one with skin hanging from it in the shape of a fish's mouth. Moving her hand from his stomach up his torso, she gave each hole a number. "One, two, there's another, three." She concluded with a final count of six.

After the count was complete, she turned dissatisfied back to the nurse. "How long ago did he come in? Where are his wife and the police?"

"The wife didn't come," the nurse explained. "Dr. Whitman came, and he's the one who talked to the police." Everyone knew this was the white man for whom Aunt Shirley worked as a maid. He owned the town, so the officers were willing to accept his explanation that his employee had shot her husband in self-defense.

The nurse leaned in to my grandmother and whispered, "If I were you, I'd file a complaint. Your son was shot with two different guns."

It was only then that Honeymoon started to go under too. She remembered the night that Uncle Rat had hit Aunt Shirley. She shook her head back and forth violently. The only sounds in the car on the ride home were those of mourning and grief.

During the week that followed, I watched as Honeymoon, in a dignified and patient manner, allowed herself to be consoled and probed. She sat in a large recliner pulled up to the spot where Uncle Rat and Aunt Shirley had always won at cards. When asked how she was feeling, she would say blankly, "Gone."

The condolence callers couldn't resist asking for more details about the shooting. They had heard odds and ends concerning the events of that night, but they knew that Honeymoon held the whole truth. In spite of her grief, she appreciated her visitors' concern and even understood their curiosity. She didn't blame them for wanting to keep such a tragedy from happening to them.

But when you're drowning, your body's responses change drastically from moment to moment. One minute Honeymoon didn't mind the intrusive questions, the next she wished everyone would go away so she could sit alone and cry. But as the days passed, she gathered herself and said, looking up at her mother, "Big Momma always said nothing good comes from a call that time of night, only whorish talk, crooked lies, and bad news. You were right about that." Then the tears came again. Baby Jane tried to escape to the front porch but was accosted by a parade of people entering the yard with family packs of Church's Chicken and Coca-Cola.

"He was lying there in his underwear, stiff as a board, a look of total surprise on his face," Honeymoon said to no one in particular. A few had the decency to turn away.

"So, girl, what do you think could have happened to cause that girl to kill that boy like that?" It was a loaded question, filled with innuendo and speculation. One spouse stabbing or shooting another was not unheard-of in Stoner Hill. People got drunk, fought, and killed one another often enough for it to be somewhat commonplace. The question they were really asking was what had Uncle Rat done to deserve it.

The night Uncle Rat hit Aunt Shirley for disappearing earlier in the day was a crucial time in their marriage, Honeymoon knew, but since she and Pappy had counseled them it had seemed the couple would make it through the rough waters. But they were just experiencing a dry drowning, their marriage corroding even as they walked around.

"The girl didn't do it by herself," Honeymoon sneered. "That boy Butch, Rat's good buddy, shot his gun too."

"What you say, child?" Honeymoon's cousin Suzy Mae stammered, pressing her Bible to her chest. "That don't sound right to me. What the police say?"

"Well, you know that boss of Shirley's owns that whole town, so he did most of the talking with the police. They say that unless I make a fuss, they're gon' accept Shirley's account and not arrest her."

"Well, what you gon' do, girl?"

"Let God work it out. That girl's got all my grandchildren to raise."

Before she could continue, Big Momma grabbed her hand. "You ain't got to worry 'bout that, honey. What's done in the dark, comes to light."

At the funeral the family squeezed into the three front rows of the church. Honeymoon, Aunt Shirley, Big Momma, and Momma sat side by side; small squares of black lace curtained their faces. Before them, beneath a picture of the Last Supper, lay Uncle Rat, in a shiny three-piece suit.

The sounds in the church were different that day. Sobs accompanied by a kind of quiet I'd never heard—no candy-paper rustles, feet shuffles, or even whispers from the pews, only a low drone escaping from the fluorescent lights. The only comfort came from the blue hydrangeas and yellow lilies that perfumed the air.

I was ten, and easily distracted in church, but that day I found myself listening painfully hard to every word that came from Pastor's lips. We were all searching for answers, for a way out of this, and I was willing to turn over a dry sermon to find it.

Uncle Rat's daughter Betty pressed her ear into my shoulder as Pastor Green looked at us and said, "This is nothing else but sorrow of the heart. Some days you will feel numb. Those will be the good ones. On others, the weight of this thing will threaten to take you under, but that's when God will lift you up."

I was vexed about something more than Uncle Rat being gone. Was it the way Uncle Rat's friend Butch let it be known around town that he and Aunt Shirley were more than just friends? Or the mortuary face powder that made Uncle Rat look like a dry fig instead of the vibrant thirty-year-old man I'd seen moving over Aunt Shirley in the dark night? Perhaps it was that stupid suit they'd put him in. I thought he should have been buried in what he died in, a T-shirt and some Fruit-of-the-Loom briefs. Resisting the pull of grief was as difficult as trying to walk on water. Pastor Green advised us to look not for answers but for the comfort of Jesus Christ.

Toward the end of the funeral the family sat upright like black crows about to rasp out their sorrow—necks stiff, throats tight, burdened yet august. Momma pleaded at the end of the service, "Let me see my brother, my brother." But just as she uttered the words, his casket was sealed. We stood and walked behind it, then watched as the sun peered down on Uncle Rat's grave.

Back at Honeymoon's a congregation of family and friends feasted on picnic fare—Cokes, fried chicken, potato salad, and pound cakes, brought over by those who'd come to pay their respects. Honeymoon had planned to continue her relationship with Aunt Shirley as if Uncle Rat's death hadn't changed things. At the burial she consoled her daughter-in-law, who cried a river. After the services, Honeymoon removed Aunt Shirley's shoes, but while serving the woman who'd killed her son coffee and tea cakes, Honeymoon felt her anger swell and she realized she couldn't tolerate Aunt Shirley's presence.

A month after Rat's death, Baby Jane answered Honeymoon's phone, listened for a voice, then started to cry, holler really. It took Honeymoon a while to calm him.

"I called Rat the night he died," he told us. "I wanted to thank him for helping me get a job after college didn't work out, and now that I'm on my feet, I wanted to get all his boys brand-new bikes for Christmas. He wasn't home from work yet. Shirley said she'd tell him to call me." Before going on, Baby Jane shrugged. We all did.

"So when you called to tell me what happened," he said, raising his eyes to meet his mother's, "I thought that you were gon' be Rat. Now whenever the phone rings, I have to remind myself that my big brother won't be calling. That time I forgot."

We all kept forgetting, then remembering, all the while treading. Momma was no exception. I watched as she tried not to let the grief take hold, but in the days after Uncle Rat's death, it gripped her the way a tick sinks into the skin and infects the whole body before it's discovered and uprooted. Momma slipped from one day into the next. During those first few months, it was my stepfather, Calvin, and his easygoing nature that kept Momma from sinking, but by the time they ate the top tier of their wedding cake to celebrate their first year anniversary, their marriage was just about over.

It took a while after Uncle Rat's death for Momma's mind to order itself once again. On a day of clarity, she decided to tackle the bills that had piled up over the last few months. It was then that she discovered the truth in what her instincts had been telling her for months.

While balancing her checkbook, she noticed among the stack of canceled checks for groceries, gas, water, and the baby's doctor visits a draft written for two hundred dollars in a handwriting not her own to a woman whose name had quickened Momma's pulse when she had heard Calvin utter it earlier. Then there was a click, as innocuous as the timer on a coffeepot, and Momma started simmering.

She was not going to be victimized the way she had been

with Jack, or destroyed like Uncle Rat. She was as strong as her mother and her mother's mother. She didn't even bother to scream. She just packed up the shaving kit she'd bought Calvin for Christmas, along with a bundle of things from his clothes drawers, and stuffed them in a plastic trash bag. In two others she dumped his fishing equipment and all the hurricane glasses collecting above the kitchen cabinets. By the time Calvin came home, Momma had lined up the three trash bags like green tepees on the curb. "It's more than you came here with," she told him.

Calvin had no place to go, so he followed Momma from room to room pleading for another chance, arguing that his son needed a man around.

For a moment Momma paused and it seemed that poor Calvin might still have a chance, but then she shook her hand at him. "My son's got men around." She looked at him over her raised hand and said, "Leave your keys, and you can put your wedding ring in the mailbox. I paid for it."

True to his listless nature, Calvin didn't put up a fuss, nor did he offer an apology or excuse. Momma just closed the door on him. But I could see from the way she leaned against the knob breathing deeply that it wasn't as easy as she made it seem. Her heavy eyelids showed her youthful vulnerability.

In the four seasons that had passed since Uncle Rat's death, the family had struggled to stay afloat. Uncle Wayne got surly, Ruby had nightmares, Baby Jane drank too much, and Momma saw the light. It was as if she'd been drowning in her own loneliness, so she'd allowed Calvin to join her even though he'd never learned to float either. After Calvin left, she stopped wishing for what she didn't have and just embraced the things that were truly hers.

At the time of my near drowning, Momma sat under a cluster of oak trees. She was spooning mashed carrots from a jar and feeding them to my baby brother while the afternoon breeze ruffled her loose blouse. I imagine her thoughts were not far from her dead brother or the husband she'd sent away. She had been watching me from her seat on a thin old quilt, and when she realized what was happening she started running with her baby on her hip toward the water.

"Yolanda!" Over the beating water and shrill laughter of my friends, I heard her call out my name.

"Yolanda, stand up, baby!" she shouted. The muscles in my chest contracted uncontrollably, and the water was suffocating me. Momma's suggestion seemed ridiculous. I could not put my mind around how standing up would do anything other than ensure that I died on my feet, but I placed my palms on the lake's soft floor, bent my legs under me, and stood until my head poked out of the water. I was shivering with terror in the hot moist air by the time Momma wrapped me with a dry towel. The children assumed I'd been playing all along.

At home that night Momma got undressed as I wondered aloud why no one had tried to help me.

"They didn't think you needed any help, baby," she said, struggling with a swollen finger. She had up to that point freed herself of everything but her wedding band. Removing it then, just before it clinked in a saucer on her dresser for the last time, she said almost to herself, "Who ever heard of someone drowning in shallow water?"

Bridges

They again did what was evil. . . . But in your great mercy
you did not put an end to them or abandon them, for
you are a gracious and merciful God.

—*Nehemiah 9:28–31*

Shreveport reclines in the northwestern corner of Louisiana. The summer before starting seventh grade, I traveled "down south" to the state's governmental and cultural core. On a Thursday morning around 4 a.m., Honeymoon, Pappy, Uncle Wayne, Donny, Michael, Ruby, and I packed into the borrowed industrial-blue van waiting for us under the streetlight to go visit my uncle William, the middle child and the troubled soul.

It always takes me a while to get around to mentioning Uncle Will. He's like the dirty panties I occasionally leave on the bathroom floor—that intimate detail I'd rather people not know. Picture a tall, dark, brooding type, towering over you in stockings and a red dress. That's one of two images my mind holds of my homosexual uncle. The other makes me ashamed.

During the first few hours of our drive, we traced the spine of the boot-shaped terrain. By the time I awoke, we were approaching the point where its toe splashes the Mississippi. The familiar farms and cotton fields had given way to bayous. There were marshy bogs in Shreveport, one behind Stoner Hill in fact, but those covered only a few blocks, while these swamps overtook the land. The highway became a succession of flat bridges. Metal beams and heavy bolts suspended the flat roads just above the water like a pier. At certain points a thick fog rose out of the water, white before us. When it was possible to see, green algae and stark trees were all that surrounded us.

Honeymoon sat in the front seat clutching a handkerchief, occasionally dabbing turpentine on her earlobes. She said it calmed her nerves, but I only noticed the aroma's impact on my ability to breathe. Honeymoon didn't like bridges, and the anxiety of the trip showed in creases on her face.

At one juncture, Ruby yapped from her rear seat, "I wonder how Will's hair looks now."

"I hope he cut it some," Honeymoon said in a faint whisper. "He should at least cut his hair and be presentable. Lord, have mercy."

Uncle Will had always presented himself differently from the rest of his family. In my grandparents' living room there was a frame about as large as the screen of a console television set. Laid out in three rows were the first-grade pictures of each of their nine children. And even at the age of six, when Uncle Will's close-cut hair was tame, that was the only cosmetic feature he shared with his brothers. While the other boys donned plaid shirts and suspenders for their school portrait, Uncle Will had chosen to wear his Easter suit and a white velvet bow tie.

While Pappy lamented over his son's hair, Michael and

Donny discussed the possibilities, then concluded that he was probably forced to wear a crew cut. At which point Uncle Wayne chided, "Will ain't in the military. He wouldn't make it there."

From narrow braids that hung down his neck to a picked-out, high-standing Afro, Uncle Will's hair stood out. It was the most outrageous, all would agree, when pressed straight with a hot comb.

"He's just always trying to get attention," Uncle Wayne added to himself.

Even in a family like ours, Uncle Will had a big personality. Over the year he'd been gone, not a Sunday went by that the senior choir director, David, didn't bemoan the absence of his star tenor and exhibitionist. Whenever David needed the Holy Ghost to catch fire, he counted on Uncle Will to lead the spirit in. I can still see Uncle Will standing in the platform heels that even men could get away with wearing in those days, shouting in an Al Green cadence, "Oh . . . He's moving! God is moving me!"

I used to laugh at his antics; only later through his letters would I understand his constant moral struggle.

I was stupid and wrong and now I'm living in a hellhole where nobody loves me [he wrote to me]. I don't fault Mom or Dad. They did their best to keep me out of this hell. I fault myself because I was hard-headed, didn't listen, left the church, left home, ran the streets with my so-called friends who don't know me now that I'm in a one-man cell trying to stay alive. I cry a lot, especially at Christmas when I can't be home with family!!! I wish I could start over from first grade again. With your momma walking me to school in the rain and making sure I stayed dry under her umbrella or playing marbles with my brothers in the back room . . .

Ruby and I had loved our adventures with Uncle Will. He often turned a boring Saturday into a day of fireworks. He'd come into Momma's house unannounced and select mix-and-match items from my closet. He'd even braid my hair. Starting at my nape, he'd tightly wind it along into a spiral honeycomb until a braided antenna hung down from the top of my head; he'd yank on this to make me erupt in laughter. After doing the same with his baby sister, Ruby, he'd carry us off to the Sears photo lab for a one-dollar set of pictures.

Uncle Will took Ruby and me to see our first movie, *Car Wash*, when it was playing at the Strand Theater on Crocket Street downtown. The theater was paneled in mahogany wood and lined with rows of sunken-in velvet chairs that smelled of mildew and buttered popcorn. It was brimming with black folks, not because of segregation—that had ceased even before I was born—but because aesthetic differences seemed to run down the color line. Everyone was talking about the movie, and Uncle Will had seen it twice already. In the boys' back room he had played the soundtrack enough times for Ruby and me to memorize the Rose Royce and Pointer Sisters songs.

Before the movie began, Uncle Will offered a summary of the story's plot. "In a nutshell," he said with a little smirk to himself, "the movie is about whether the skinny little boy with the Afro will ever get a date with the stuck-up, wannabe-white waitress and if the fat-headed ex-con with the burnt lips will be able to keep from going back to jail." Toward the end of the movie, we were sitting comfortably in our chairs—Uncle Will on the end, next to him Ruby, then me, when Uncle Will shouted out, "I'm them, they're me," referring to the characters and their hard-knock, meager lives. Uncle Will—who had dropped out of high school a few years earlier and had suffered numerous indignities as a menial hamburger cook, Ferris wheel repairman, and car washer—understood self-inflicted tragedy all too well. Several times Ruby and I looked up to see tears streaking his cheeks.

After the movie Uncle Will opened the driver's side of Pappy's handed-down Pinto and said, "Which of my sister girls wants to try first?" I was half afraid, but Ruby jumped right into the driver's seat, shouting, "Me, me, me." Uncle Will had been letting us "drive" since we were old enough to sit in his lap and see over the top of the steering wheel. I could never keep the car on the road, but by now Ruby could get us all the way home. Momma and Honeymoon would have strung him up by his earrings if they had known, but of course we never told. Uncle Will trusted that children would never tell anything.

Uncle Will sat on the passenger side, giving the fourteen-year-old instructions. "Turn it steady, Ruby. You got it. You got it!" he cheered. Ruby and Uncle Will maneuvered the car toward the backside of downtown, known appropriately as "the Bottom"—a cluster of filthy streets where dirty wet clothes hung from wire lines as half-clothed babies, mostly unattended, crawled beneath. At night houses doubled as prostitute dens, red nipple-shaped lights winking to customers, "Come in."

Uncle Will started waving his hand outside the car window the moment he caught sight of one of his girls—another cross-dressing friend. This one wore a giant sunflower stuck behind his left ear. The rest of the outfit—a halter top fitted above jeans pulled too high up on the waist—looked clownish but did not confound Ruby and me. We had grown accustomed to the pe-culiar dress of Uncle Will and his friends.

Uncle Will's girlfriend asked to come along with us back to Honeymoon's house, and Uncle Will obliged. Ruby pulled her brother's hand to get him to say no. She knew that if anyone caught this fake-eyelash spectacle in the back room there would be hell to pay.

Just a few weeks earlier, Baby Jane had walked in to find Uncle Will in makeup prancing his six-foot frame around the room in a rose-print dress stuffed with falsies. Startled, Baby Jane called his brother a ghetto punk. Uncle Will, smacking his own butt in the air, piped to his brother, "Kiss it." Which Baby Jane did with a swift kick.

The lipstick and dresses were not the only things about Uncle Will that enraged his brothers. It was just one more thing fueling the flame that Uncle Will, the hell-raiser, kept ablaze. My lost uncle could quickly move from being silly and carefree to being just plain low-down. Shortly after Uncle Rat was killed, Will faked his own death to see if people would care as much. The night after Jack shot Momma, Uncle Will had crawled through Momma's bedroom window to steal her rent money while she lay in the hospital trying not to bleed to death. Honeymoon kept warning him that he was headed for trouble, but she never suspected it would be of the sort that required her to bridge a hundred miles of water, disappointment, and shame, then have to park on the deck of a ferry that stretched out like a parking lot and hold her breath while the boat slowly swung to the rhythm of the Mississippi.

"Oooh, I don't know if I'm gon' make it," Honeymoon said, holding the turpentine under her neck.

"We almost there, Honey. You'll be fine," Pappy said, slapping her on the thigh. Giant gray-and-white seagulls swooped down and back up again.

The ferry docked on an island that had just appeared after we turned a bend in the river. Pappy steered the car over another narrow bridge, then down several back roads. Finally we spotted the tower and high walls that surrounded Angola State Penitentiary. The guards who carried cold black guns and wore matching charcoal gray uniforms escorted us from the parking lot to a bus that would take us and the other people, who'd been waiting inside the gates, for a visit with our loved ones. The prison was arranged like a small college campus with military-style barracks dotting the grounds. The bus unloaded us at what was called the "canteen," where we waited at a large bolted-down wooden table for Uncle Will to appear.

I remembered the day the police came to get him. I was just approaching my teens and becoming sensitive to what others thought of me, but I still enjoyed swinging from Pappy's pear trees. By the thick of summer, as I reached from one limb to the next, the leaves fanned and sang like maracas. The police appeared from the adjoining backyards, black pistols cocked, warning, "Get down and don't move."

They kicked in the boys' back door and came out with Uncle Will, unshaven, with half his hair flailing from the shakeup, the other side braided into chains. I looked from my uncle to the neighbors who'd come out of their houses to watch. Honeymoon and Pappy, distraught, hurried after the police cruisers.

There was no open talk that night about what had happened, but Uncle Will had by this time accumulated a long list of offenses. Though most were against the family, there had been the sense long before that it was only a matter of time before the young man would venture out.

The day following his arrest, there was a brief mention of

Uncle Will in the paper. Only a few words were written, but they told a horrible story.

SHREVEPORT MAN ARRESTED

A 24-year-old Shreveport man was charged with aggravated rape in connection with a homosexual assault of a 9-year-old boy. Investigator Albert Luke and Shreveport officers armed with a fugitive warrant arrested the man Tuesday in his home. He was in the custody of Bossier deputies Wednesday, placed in the parish jail in Bossier where he confessed to the charges. A sheriff's office spokesman said the boy was enticed into a car near his home by a man who offered him money. The man drove to a waste field, where the boy was sexually assaulted and abandoned.

No one in the family directly addressed Uncle Will's crime. They probably felt, as I did, that it was really too evil a thing to let lie on the mind. So when Uncle Will, in ankle chains, appeared from a metal door in crisp blue jeans and a pressed white T-shirt, we talked about everything but what he had done. When he gathered us in his arms, we returned his embrace.

"You look real good, Mom," he said, stepping back to observe her the way he had most Sundays. She couldn't say the same for him after touching the deep cuts and scratches marring his face. As if reading her mind, Uncle Will offered, "You don't know what I have to do to survive in here." Then he dropped into a chair and began to cry.

"Now, now, Will," Honeymoon said, patting her son on the back. "Stop all that." Pappy seconded her command. The rest of us just looked down.

Then, to change the subject and bring some dignity back to

his brother, Uncle Wayne offered, "Looks like the Orioles got a chance this year." Uncle Will nodded, remembered his place among our clan of men, and straightened his back.

"Come here, Yolanda," Uncle Will eventually called to me. "Let me see what you're wearing." I approached slowly, a little afraid at first, but then he spun me around. "Girl, you've grown in a year." Smiling, he turned to his baby sister. "Now, you, Ruby, show me what you've got." On cue Ruby started dancing the hustle, and we all laughed like it was old times.

When it was time for us to leave, Uncle Will turned intently to his parents. "Do you still love me?" he asked, already in tears.

"Yes, precious baby," Honeymoon said, rubbing the water from his cheeks. "You never have to worry about that."

"We hate the sin, son, but we still love the sinner," Pappy said.

The statement seemed contradictory to me, but I waited until we'd crossed all the bridges on the way back home before I asked, "Hate the sin, love the sinner? How do you do that?"

"It's very hard, little one," Honeymoon said. "Very hard." She thought on it for a few moments, then added, "I love my son, but he went and ruined another child's life. I don't like that, just like I don't like crossing bridges. But for the sake of my son, I've got to close my eyes, calm my nerves, and pass on over it."

"No matter what, Honeymoon?" I asked.

She stretched her arms out to the road ahead and reassured me, "I'd cross bridges for any of you—no matter what."

I Don't Want to Go to
May-hee-co, No, No, No!

He watches over the foreigners; he sustains the fatherless and the
widow; but the way of the wicked, he turns upside down.

—*Psalms 146:9*

The swelter season that preceded the start of junior high school
went by idly, with me poised staring blankly before our wood-
framed console television set. In a departure from previous
summers of afternoons watching *All My Children* and *The Edge
of Night*, my days were often interrupted by special news bul-
letins concerning the American hostages in Iran and the accu-
mulation of dead black boys in Atlanta.

At night I was compelled to watch the movie *The Late Great
Planet Earth* on HBO over and over again. One word, like a
tolling bell, describes that summer to me: "ominous." Ominous
was the thunderous voice of Orson Welles in cinematic apoca-
lypse; so was the tension that surrounded the cold war and the
Shreveport Board of Education's vote to close our junior high
and bus my fellow classmates and me to a white school. To-

gether, these events gripped me like the shadow of death. I was, at eleven years old, certain the world was coming to an end.

I kept this idea to myself, since in the past after such revelations, I had been ridiculed and mocked. Like the time my youngest uncle, Michael, caught me eating the red berries from Honeymoon's holly bush. "Girl, what you doing?" he'd said, wide eyes of concern masking his mischief. "Don't you know that's poison?"

I quickly surveyed his demeanor, searching for an eye twitch or ear wiggle to offer a hint of his ruse. Michael stared back at me somberly, playing me with the skill he often used to win three corners in a game of tic-tac-toe. I opened my mouth and hollered. The berries cascaded down my chin in wet, mushy clumps.

"No need crying now. You 'bout to die. Go on in the house and tell everybody bye," Michael said while scooting me up the steps to the porch. I cried the rest of the day and into the night. There was nothing Momma or Honeymoon could say or do to convince me that I wasn't going to grow cold and hard with my next breath.

And five years later, I took Mr. Welles's prediction of doom even more seriously than I had Michael's cockeyed fabrication because, as the narrator portended, "There were signs!" that multiplied like mumps at the community pool. The same way one child comes home early complaining of a headache, then before long everyone is walking around with sardine-stuffed handkerchiefs tied to their faces, that summer, one omen piled on top of another.

After about my third viewing of the *The Late Great Planet Earth*, I ascertained that foreigners—Russians, Arabs, and Asians, in particular—would initiate the world's impending destruction. I understood our suspicions concerning the Russians and Iranians, since each group—the Russians with their long-range nuclear weapons and the machine-gun-toting Iranian militants demanding the Shah in exchange for their fifty-three American prisoners—was holding our country hostage. It was the unrelenting admonition concerning the evils of the "yellow peril" that I couldn't understand. Apparently the Chinese were gathering late at night in remote caves plotting to take over the world. My knowledge of them was limited, which made it easy to paint them as the enemy.

A few days after the Americans were captured, the Iranians released the blacks and women, probably reasoning that they were powerless victims. This act incited more gloom among my kin. As Big Momma's sister put it while emptying coffee grinds out of a tin pot, "Even folks who don't bathe know women and niggas don't mean nothing to whitey. Worthless is what we are." When I asked her in response if she thought the world was coming to an end, she just said, "Could be," and started snapping the ends off green beans.

As a Christian, I should have been eagerly anticipating the sounding of the trumpet that would announce the return of Christ. But in truth, though I loved the Lord and appreciated Jesus dying for my sins, the thought of his face blazing across the sky and signaling the end of all time scared the pee out of me.

With knowledge that the Russians had enough nuclear warheads to blow America away a hundred times, that the Iranians were about to force us into a war, and that some nigger-hater was killing black children and dumping them in wooded lots all over Atlanta, you'd think that the women in our neighborhood would have had enough worries to feast on, but their teeth were sunk into the Caddo Parish School Board's decision to close Valencia Junior High School. On the day of the board's vote, to themselves they whispered, "Whitey is evil and selfish as the day is long. How they gon' take babies, some as young as ten years old, and send them away from their neighborhood to go to school?" Out loud they whooped and hollered that we needed the traditions and nurturing of our own before being exposed to the real world—the white world. The white men who sat on the board told them to stop overreacting. This wasn't the sort of forced integration that Uncle Wayne had endured six years earlier. It wouldn't be hostile. "The change will be good for Stoner Hill," the school officials said, not understanding why our parents wanted us to stay on the poor side of town. "Your children will be challenged."

But will they be accepted? our mothers wondered.

I don't know if it was due to Big Momma's recollection of a boss man who encouraged a speedier cotton picking by whacking her knuckles with a stick, Uncle Wayne's mistreatment at Byrd High, or the way store managers stared at me but I had to admit, I didn't trust white people. Aside from the few white teachers who worked at Stoner Hill and the missionaries who used to come into the neighborhood dressed like calico hippies singing "Jolly Bible Time," the closest I ever got to white people was waiting for Honeymoon outside her boss's house. So on the first day of school, I expected the beginning of the end.

At the bus stop on the corner of East Kings Highway and Youree Drive, I squinted at the sun that was making moisture stick to me like hot wax and waited for the sky to part and the sound of trumpets proclaiming Jesus' arrival. Instead, I was startled by the buzz of the bus that quieted to a hum as its doors opened.

Wobbling down the aisle, I tripped over a leg and a *Star Wars* backpack before finding a seat next to Fizz. Our only experience riding a school bus had been on supervised field trips, but no teachers were present to settle us down as we rode out of our weedy neighborhood of faded houses and started down East Kings Highway.

The blacks and whites of Shreveport had mastered the art of living together separately. Early city designs took a lack of transportation into account and planned for every grand neighborhood built for whites to have a few nearby shacks to accommodate the blacks working in them. Entering the wealthy Shreve Highland neighborhood, we kids all pressed our faces against the windows and admired the manicured backyards. There was nothing mundane about them—even the trees were grand. My own grandfather had been among those hired to replace the common pines and oaks with fluffy white Bradford pear trees that waved feathery white blooms in the spring air and turned hot red in fall. Swimming pools, tennis courts, and grass as thick and even as a shag carpet filled us with longing.

"That one's mine," Teresa yelled out. We each went on to claim one of those colonial two-story homes. With pillars as tall as trees, they were a far cry from our leaky-roofed shotguns. Though the two neighborhoods were separated only by backyards, each had its own elementary school, so the younger children almost never went to school together. As the bus drew nearer to our new school, our nervous energy overtook us, and we threw back our heads, pounced on the black leather seats, and chanted a playground song.

> I don't want to go to May-hee-co,
> No, no, no.

There's a big policeman at the
Do', do', do'.
He'll take you by the collar,
Make you pay a dollar.
See what I mean,
Jelly bean?
He'll wash your face in gasoline.
He'll make you eat a snake,
Jump in the lake,
And come out with a bellyache.

May-hee-co just meant someplace little black kids didn't know and were afraid of. It could have been Russia, Iran, or, in our case, the ugly square building where we'd learn during seventh and eighth grades.

"Y'all know they sending us over here to get killed like them black boys in Atlanta," Jason said, with uncharacteristic nervousness.

"For real?" asked Dwight, biting his pencil.

"No, not for real," I answered, clinking the dimes inside my right jean pocket. "Jason's just talking." Honeymoon had given them to me the day before with a warning: "You keep two dimes with you everywhere you go. If anything happens, you call me or your momma. See, I ain't got nothing against them personal, but living has taught me you always got to watch whitey."

Jason looked at me sideways, the faintest signs of a mustache shadowing his lips. "Girl, don't you know it's a white man out there stripping black kids down and then dumping their dead bodies in the woods?" I turned away, biting my lips, and joined in another round of our song:

other races. Ann thought her school-imposed nickname, "Super A," referenced her first name. It sometimes seemed to me a way of suggesting Ann's only motivation was to be number one. "She's the school worker bee," I once overheard a teacher say.

In the halls of Broadmoor those first days, I noticed that the way the white boys walked, straight up and down with a slight bounce, differed from that of my boys, who glided from side to side, hands in their pockets, shoulders lowered. The girls made a habit of swinging their long, soft hair behind their shoulder blades. Their sentences began with words like "actually" and "perhaps," and they made statements sound like questions. My friends had flamboyant monikers like Lakesha, Shatosha, and Garnell, while my new peers had names as bland as their complexions—everyone was a John, Kim, or Thomas. The locker room smelled of them, like the wet leaves used in salad. And as we changed into our T-shirts, I noticed only a couple of the girls needed the bras that I'd been wearing since I was nine years old. It was rude, but I stared because they were white people, different from me in every way. The administration maintained this distinction by advancing the notion that the white kids were smarter. It was done subtly, but this opinion showed itself most clearly in the division of our classes.

Even before the Stoner Hill children arrived, three distinct learning groups had been established—the slow kids, who read from large-print books and played learning games all day; the gifted students, who were required to write papers on the meaning of works like *The Diary of Anne Frank* and Edgar Allan Poe's "The Raven"; and the leftovers, who were dumped into large classes and labeled "general." As Ann had told me, her arms defiantly swaying, instead of determining placement by grades, test scores, and Stoner Hill teacher recommendations, Broadmoor's counselors had determined the black students were as similar as paper clips and swept all of us into general classes. When the secretary said she couldn't budge, Ann suggested a school protest, though I wasn't about to wait on her. Honeymoon had been right. You did have to watch whitey.

Being smart was how I had come to see myself, but as I walked out the office and down the hallway to where two narrow metal pay phones were mounted, I worried: *What if they're right and I'm not smart enough to keep up with these white kids?* I shook off the doubt, picked up the receiver, and did the only thing I knew to do—I called my mother.

Now, Momma was known for having a quiet, ladylike demeanor, soft voice, and gentle nature, but there was something else people picked up about Momma right off: when it came to her children, she didn't take no mess. As it happened, she was already planning a visit to Broadmoor that night for the first parent-teacher meeting, and she strode into the gymnasium, determined to get to the bottom of all this. Looking over the crowd, Momma spotted Mr. Heard, the principal, standing in a square blue suit at center court. She made her way to him and stood nose-to-nose with the squat white man.

After briefly listening to Momma's concern, Mr. Heard interrupted her with a curt "I'll look into it tomorrow." The moment he let the last syllable go, he realized his mistake because now the curly-haired woman clutching a PTA program was glaring at him and ready to explode. When she did, silence fell around her. It was the moment every child dreads. If given a choice, I'd rather have spent the rest of the school year stacking Lego blocks than witness the embarrassing exchange taking place. Momma's voice rose to a level that made my ears ring. Parents stared, and Mr. Heard's face bled a shamed red.

"No, you'll look into it now!" she demanded. "Who do you

think you're policing? You've kept my child out of her rightful classes." Stretching the red nail tip of her index finger to within an inch of Mr. Heard's nose, Momma lowered her voice to an even more threatening register and said, "I pay your salary with my tax dollars like all these other people in here. I'm telling you that my child has a problem, and right now is when it will be solved!"

Mr. Heard scurried Momma and me off to his office to review my file. It took only a cursory review of my records for my new principal to realize his placement committee had made a mistake. In addition to changing my schedule, he told Momma he'd review the other children's records within the week.

In the car on the way home, I reiterated Honeymoon's words: "Yep, you do have to watch whitey."

To that Momma reached over and smacked me on the forehead. "You just watch yourself," she said.

The next day Mr. Heard called me into his office to apologize. The following week he beckoned me in the hall.

"Mrs. Laurel says you put a different spin on the topics you discuss in her history class," he said, smiling as he examined me over the top of his glasses. This was the day after I'd opined to the class that Columbus was no different from Kunta Kinte's Massa Reynolds.

This sort of chitchat went on between my principal and me for a few more weeks before Mr. Heard hatched a curious scheme. Leaning over his desk toward me in a conspiratorial manner, the gray-haired man propositioned, "Listen, Yolanda. You're a smart, intuitive girl, and I need you to keep an eye on things around here for me."

"Like a mole?" I asked, rearing back in my chair and watching him suspiciously. Mr. Heard's way of doing things concerned me. Looked at closely—the bushy hair, the short, stocky frame, the red cheeks and nose—he seemed to favor a Russian ancestry. Sensing my apprehension, he quickly explained that rather than spying, I'd be sharing my observations of how everyone was getting along. I agreed and soon reported that black and white kids sat on opposite sides of the cafeteria and didn't talk to one another outside of class.

Once my eyes were open, I made other discoveries. The world didn't end, and in January the Iranian hostages were released after a lengthy delay orchestrated by American politicians. A few months later a black man was charged with the Atlanta killings, which suddenly stopped after his arrest. After citizens of the United States and Soviet Union shared their similar desire for good schools, state-of-the-art hospitals, and, most important, peace, at a satellite town-hall-style meeting on *Donahue*, I thought anything was possible. If people separated by half a planet had similar goals, surely there was a way for black and white kids at Broadmoor to come together.

When I shared my revelation with Mr. Heard, he asked what I was going to do about it.

"You're the white man. You tell me," I cracked. We had come to joke like this.

Eventually I decided to run for student council and composed a three-minute speech outlining the duties I'd undertake—conduct biweekly meetings, oversee school fund-raisers, and attend school sports competitions. Ann listened, then told me I didn't stand a chance.

"No," she insisted, nibbling on a dish of cold cabbage, "you sound like all the others. No one remembers that." Ann's family had immigrated to the United States before her birth, so while she usually spoke in long sentences laced in a mild Southern drawl, she sometimes reverted to the choppy English she heard at home in the same manner that I occasionally sprinkled "ain't" and "yo' " into my speech at school. Perhaps her native meal, which tasted like the pickled vegetables in Big Momma's "cha-cha," sent her swirling back to old customs.

Insulted, I stared at her as she continued to grind pickled green morsels between her braces.

"You care about that?" she asked, tapping my paper with her fork and ignoring my disdainful glare.

"Yeah," I defended.

"Well, no one else does. You want to win," she said, almost jabbing the pointed utensil into my chest, "you write something from here."

Ann's frank critique reminded me of being a little girl again. Since I could remember, Big Momma had been helping me recite Scriptures. "Jesus wept," I'd learned around the time I took my first steps. I had never found it hard to memorize Bible verses. They were as familiar to me as my reflection in the mirror, even more so really, because they were everywhere I looked. Small quotes like "Jesus lives" and "The Lord is my shepherd" were etched into little crystal ornaments that sat in Big Momma's picture windows. "They that wait upon the Lord shall renew their strength" was embroidered on the doily adorning her living room chair. One Christmas I received a pillow cushion stitched with "The meek shall inherit the earth."

Before I reached past Big Momma's hip, I was using large words and exaggerated gestures for greater emphasis in my Scripture readings at church. The ladies in their feather hats would smile and clap on cue while their male counterparts removed square white hankerchiefs from their breast pockets and waved "amens" my way. I loved the attention and the proud look on Big Momma's face when she said, "Londa, that was beautiful, girl."

One Youth Sunday, when I was eight or nine, Big Momma had made an ambitious selection of the entire Psalm 119 for me to memorize and recite. When the day came, I bounced up to the pulpit in white patent leather shoes so new they possessed not a single scuff or scratch. My head was adorned in fresh Shirley Temple curls, and I was ready to woo the crowd, but having been remiss in my memorization of the psalm's 176 verses, I was wholly unprepared. I opened my mouth to begin, but I could not remember a single word. Big Momma, in a loud whisper, quoted the opening line: "Blessed are they whose ways are blameless, and who walk according to the law of the Lord."

I picked up there for a few verses but soon stumbled again. "With my whole heart I have sought thee," Big Momma assisted, stretching as far forward as she could while still remaining in her pew.

"Thy word have I hid in my heart," I repeated, my fingers crunched together in a ball on my lap, my voice trembling. The speech became a two-way play between Big Momma and me and ended with me leaving the podium to bury my face in Big Momma's breasts. "I'm sorry, Big Momma. I'm so sorry," I repeated through tears of shame and embarrassment.

"That's okay, baby," she assured me later. "It's my fault. I forgot to tell you, that these ain't just words. This thang has got to be in your heart." For Big Momma, what she spoke from that black book wasn't just words on a page. As she explained it, the things that come out of our mouths should originate from deep within us. "When that thang's in your heart," Big Momma said, "you won't forget it."

On the day of the election, I sat on the gymnasium floor with students running for school mascot, the cheerleading team, and the student council offices. Over the bleachers, light poured through the windows and cast a pall over individual faces. I could only make out a pattern of black and white, the darker students clumped together like shaded buildings against a cloudy-white sky. We were strangers to one another. Our bodies didn't move the same way, words slipped differently from our tongues. As the cheerleader tryouts began, I saw that even our clothes shouted our differences.

The white candidates from Shreve Island wore pastel-colored polo shirts with matching tennis skirts. Their cheerleading routines, rendered in a hoarse, choppy cadence, were punctuated by grand jetés and split jumps, one scissor leap after another. Then the black girls came up and performed singsongy dance routines in which their arms flared out over their heads with hips rocking back and forth. Their idea of a finale was a series of cartwheels. Seeing the contrasts bothered me tremendously, and so did the nagging admission that I could only make within myself—that the white girls had looked sharper, cleaner, even prettier to me, and considering that we were well outnumbered, I feared we didn't stand much of a chance.

As I listened to the other candidates, I realized that Ann had been right. Even such an experienced candidate as Kimberly Wrye spoke dryly about her family's accomplishments—her father's seat on the city council, their civic endeavors and commitment to certain charities. Like the other speeches, it was neither original nor stirring.

The only unique speech was offered by a skinny brown girl, with an endless array of ribbons cascading down a drove of ponytails.

"I'm Shameka Jackson," she said, "and I want to be a student representative. I is ready for the challenge. I'm like this glove," she said, waving a baseball mitt. "I'm ready to catch anything y'all throw my way." While the white kids looked on in respectful silence, the boys from her neighborhood shouted from the bleachers, "Shameka ain't got on no panties. Shameka ain't got no daddy." Shameka looked over in the boys' direction and screamed, "Shut up, stupids," then, looking straight ahead again with a nervous smile, she closed: "Sorry 'bout that, y'all. Vote for me, Shameka Jackson." Apparently, whitey was not the only one we needed to watch. In that moment I was grateful for Ann's admonishment and Big Momma's wise ministrations.

When it was my turn at the podium, I looked up past the metal rafters to where the sun showered through square glass panes onto the gymnasium floor. With the warm heat on my face I began by reciting one of Big Momma's familiar Bible refrains.

" 'Am I my brother's keeper?' And who is my brother anyway? Is he my blood? Is he my neighbor or my friend? Is he my enemy or someone I think so little of I don't even bother to know?

"I have asked myself these questions every day since I've been here. Before the school day begins, I stand unnoticed on the sidewalk huddled with a couple of kids I've known all my life and watch as strangers pass us by. I wonder, 'Will they ever see me?'

"For those of you who don't know me, my name is Yolanda Young, and I'd like to be your next vice president. And I declare in answer to the question 'Am I my brother's keeper?' Yes, I am.

"I don't only think of the little boy with whom I share a home. I include in my family the kids I travel with by bus every morning and my classroom neighbors as well. Listen, we all come from different houses. Some are sprawling Tudors that can hold as many people as some churches. There are some houses on my block that resemble pencil boxes. We can look at that as a big difference, or we can put it in the context of where we sit right now—next to one another. Ten years from now, no matter where we live, we will all be from this place. Do you want to look back and realize you don't know your family at all? I believe that deep down we all feel that we are our brother's keeper. We just need to get to know one another."

When I finished my speech there was loud applause, smiles, and "Great job"s from surprised black friends and white strangers alike. Fortunately, the election was held that day while emotions still ran high. I won, and so did two of the black cheerleaders, but they were limited victories. Over the last few weeks of school, I saw the first stirrings of change. The white quarterback who exchanged plays and jokes with his black receivers over spaghetti. We watched the cheerleaders, both black and white, build towers on one another's shoulders.

The year ended without any of the dramatic flair with which it had opened. I spent the last days of my seventh grade trying to get to know the other elected school officers and change myself. I didn't wait for my teachers to recognize me; instead, I shouted out to them from across the hall. For me the most surprising thing to happen that year was my finding in Ann Chang an ally when I'd expected a foe.

Darkness for Light

Woe to those who call evil good and good evil, who
put darkness for light and light for darkness, who put
bitter for sweet and sweet for bitter.

—Isaiah 5:20

"What is it that causes us to withdraw from the light and suc-
cumb to the darkness?"

It was a question as suited to Deacon Gardner as the self-
tailored jacket and brown trousers he wore on Sundays. Only
one thing enthused the studied and disciplined man, brought
him to his knees and his students to their feet: revelation.

Every Sunday evening at five-thirty I sat, straight up or
hunched down, depending on my mood, reading, underlining,
and writing in my Bible's margins the redemptive principles of
Christian doctrine as dictated by the retired military man. Beside me on the back pew were the deacon's son, Shel, and a flat-
footed girl named Tonya. Farther down were a menacing batch
of boys and a quick girl named Tammy who sparred in sharp
word exchanges with Ruby. Our parents insisted we attend St.

Peter's evening church study, so we resigned ourselves to being there and tried to make the most of it.

In that humble place of worship, where the overhead lights flickered and the newly installed air conditioners couldn't decide whether to blow out hot air or cold, Deacon Gardner wasted no time on such weightless matters as, say, the infraction in eating swine or working on the Sabbath. "Let's get to the heart of it" was his usual refrain.

While up front at the Communion table the ushers discussed next Sunday's post designations and small children stumbled about, our back-pew group of hyper teens fixed ourselves on Deacon Gardner. He believed that anyone could be enlightened, even us. He himself had received no formal education beyond high school but had searched out knowledge independently with the aid of a well-used library card. Without the emotional foot-stomping fervor typical of church leaders, Deacon Gardner pursued this contemplative questioning. "Don't you young people find it curious that even though light is associated with joy and goodness, there are those who prefer the darkness?" He smiled knowingly. "Young people don't find this phenomenon interesting at all. You are curious about other things, and there's nothing wrong with that." Walking a few paces down the row, Deacon Gardner stopped in front of the boys and retrieved a clear peppermint wrapper from the floor.

"You young people are at the age in which the body becomes ripe and the mind craves answers. Explore. Read everything you can, but only to quench your curiosity, not to satisfy your flesh." He stopped and gathered our eyes. "There are only three ways in which Satan can trap you." With that statement, Deacon Gardner captured us. Three simple and easy shortcuts to the Kingdom were what we craved. Our teacher held up three fingers, one at a time. "Lust of the flesh, lust of the eye, pride of life. Every infraction we commit against our Holy Father can be traced back to one of these three."

This had been true from the beginning, Deacon Gardner insisted. Why had Eve eaten the forbidden fruit? Satan had pinched her insecurity. Eve wanted the pride of knowing. With her husband it was the lust of the flesh. Adam knew that to get what he wanted, he must first acquiesce. And for their son Cain, it was lust of the eye, the way in which Cain coveted the blessings of his brother enough to kill him. In his case, the darkness won out.

As the modest suit buttons and dead-straight hems suggested, Deacon Gardner was a conservative and deliberate man. In the Air Force he had learned to sew with a precision that suited his scrupulous nature. This right-minded disposition also led our class to toil mercilessly for an entire month over the fifty words that make up the first six verses of the book of Genesis. Instead of raking over sentences, he examined each individual word, lifting it to the light as he would a blade of grass. "Why did the author choose 'and' instead of 'but' to connect the last clause in the second verse? . . . Can someone define for me please the meaning of the word 'light'? . . . Is there any other way to mark the passage of time besides the rotation of day and night?" It was not only his questions that attended to the slightest detail. Just as precise were his illuminations on the sun's density, the speed at which light traveled, and the reasons why it could occasionally be eclipsed. Deacon Gardner was constantly searching out the soft spot in our heads in order to plant something there.

"Why didn't God just keep us in darkness?" he asked one Sunday, coyly brushing his thinly sheared mustache.

"So that we could see?" one of the boys at the end of the pew suggested, pleased with his simple answer. Deacon Gardner smiled, then asked the question again. Eyes darted to avoid his.

Demonstrating his willing patience, Deacon Gardner allowed the silence to persist for a few moments longer before adding, "The sun and light provide us with direction, warmth, and protection. Light is a metaphor used often in the Bible to refer to God and Jesus Christ. Perhaps it would be helpful if you were to recall some of those passages." Looking at me, he said, "David said in Psalm 27 what, Yolanda?"

" 'The Lord is my light and my salvation,' " I answered, delighted to trumpet my psalm learning. Deacon Gardner then cited John's reference to God as a light unto his path to demonstrate that only in the light can we find our way.

"Haven't you noticed," he suggested to no one in particular, "that bad things tend to happen more at night? Cars get broken into. People get shot or stabbed. Businesses are robbed. We even cry more at night."

A shadow was falling over the church—an indication to me that Deacon Gardner's lecture was once again dragging past the allotted time. My gestures to leave did not escape him.

"Yolanda," he called out to me without the slightest hint of annoyance, "you're gathering your things up to leave before class lets out. You know, an impatient farmer never reaps a good harvest."

School had recently recessed for summer vacation, and Deacon Gardner, having a child my age, knew that meant Sunday was Black Night at the skating rink. Not that we couldn't go on a Friday or Saturday night, but we preferred the pulse of rhythm and blues to barbershop songs. It was not often that Momma let me go, so I told the deacon that I was eager to join my friend Fizz and her older brother waiting outside for me in his car.

"Why don't you invite them in?" Deacon Gardner asked earnestly.

Fizz didn't go to church, and I said so.

"So, you're a part of two worlds while they stay true to theirs?" he asked, propping his foot on the edge of the pew. "Next Sunday I want you to wear what you would to the skating rink, and when your friends pull up, invite them to come inside. We will then spend the entire class engaged in the sort of discussion you young people carry on when you're by yourselves."

Looking at the deacon, his arms folded stiffly, I couldn't imagine how he would respond to our lengthy discussions concerning the meaning of Rick James's lyrics in "Super Freak," Fizz's brother's obsession with *Playboy* magazine, or the consequences of wearing no panties underneath our jeans. I thanked Deacon Gardner profusely for the invitation but suggested that it wasn't a good idea.

"Why?" he asked in a voice tinged with an Alabama drawl. "You see, young people, that is my point. In here"—for dramatic emphasis Deacon Gardner gazed slowly around the church—"you're under a watchful eye. Out there"—he pointed to a window—"it's just you and Satan, if you forget to take God."

Deacon Gardner liked ending on such proverbial zingers, so he clasped his hands behind his back and began to pray, "May the Lord."

The class responded in kind, "May the Lord."

"Watch between."

"Watch between."

"Me and Thee. While we're absent. One from another. Amen."

There was a scramble for the door.

Out front the sun was still hanging over the western sky. Reclining in the driver's seat of a white gas-guzzler was Fizz's brother Sebastian. He wore tinted sunglasses crafted in cat-shaped plastic frames, and a white terry-cloth sweatband wrapped around his head. His T-shirt sleeves were rolled up to his shoulders, revealing lanky arms. Fizz was leaning out the passenger window trying to stop sweat from ruining her hair. I jumped in the backseat and immediately began pulling on my Levi's underneath my skirt.

"What's up?" Sebastian asked, looking forward. I muttered a brief answer while tussling to remove my skirt.

Watching me through the rearview mirror, Fizz mused about her day. "Girl, I had to pull a little drama in the Fitzpatrick household to get to wear these," she said, lifting her butt off the car seat to show me the gold signature threaded into her jeans. It was her practice to plan her Sunday-evening attire at the start of the day. While I busied myself at church with Scripture readings and a stirring rendition of "What a Friend We Have in Jesus," she had been eyeing her older sister's denims, but Pearl would not consign them. Fizz started screaming about not having anything or anyone to rely on. A brawl ensued, by the end of which Fizz lay dazed and denimless on the floor. Luckily, her oldest sister, Kim, took pity on her and let Fizz borrow a brand-new pair of Gloria Vanderbilt jeans.

I envied Fizz's freedom. Although she lived with her mother and nine siblings in the confined corners of her grandmother's two-bedroom house, her life had no boundaries. I, on the other hand, with my own bedroom, phone line, and closets, had nothing but. Even to get permission to go to the skating rink on a Sunday took a week's worth of pleading, some tears, and a few responsible words to my mother from Sebastian, whose mild manner and maturity even Momma admired.

With all his family's moves, Sebastian's poor school-attendance record forced him to repeat a year of grade school. This didn't prevent him from getting a driver's license the day he turned fifteen. He had a job cleaning commercial buildings, and like Deacon Gardner, Sebastian didn't need a teacher to tell him he was smart. He read everything from the jokes inside bubble gum wrappers to the stock prices in *The Wall Street Journal*s he found in the office trash. He was also an ingenious listener, able to make out all the notes in a musical chord or the problem with his engine when it wheezed.

Although Fizz and I were only going to the eighth grade, Sebastian let us follow him around. When Momma was agreeable, we'd party at the Progressive Men's Club, which—contrary to its name—was a teen dance hall that sold Shastas and Moon Pies at the front door. Sebastian never danced, insisting that he'd come to observe. All night he would stand against a wall in the windowless warehouse, nodding approval at the track selections of the robust deejay, Jabber Jaws, and his tar baby sidekick, Juberry. Another time he took us to a concert at the Hirsh Memorial Coliseum but was disappointed when Rick James declined the audience's request that he light a cigar-size joint onstage.

In the car now Sebastian popped a tape into the cassette player he'd just installed, and a witchy sound took over.

"What's that?" I asked, leaning up from the backseat.

"Jazz, baby." Sometimes Sebastian thought he was too cool. "That doesn't sound like the Dorsey Summerfield Quartet to me," I said, referring to the local group that favored Duke Ellington and Louis Armstrong tunes. This sound was new.

"This is Miles and Coltrane, kid. Wise up." Sebastian shot me a grin. The music sounded devilish—violent, wicked, and sassy all at once. Beneath the hypnotic foreplay of the heaving saxophone and howling trumpet, Fizz was still going on about her jeans.

Following the music and the colors it made in my mind while pretending to listen, I rested my eyes on the sparkles of sweat cresting on the tip of her nose. Reassured, Fizz went on. "Nearly drowned them in starch, and instead of the regular iron, I used Granny's old black one." I didn't own a pair of expensive designer jeans. Momma said Levi's were the best jeans you could have, so I rotated three pairs of them.

On the way to the rink, Sebastian stopped at the 7-Eleven to kill the remaining daylight. A fat white man stood like a Navy cook behind the counter, overhead vents blowing his hair out of place.

"You got *Playboy*?" Sebastian slurred, a toothpick locked tightly between his side teeth.

The cashier held the book up and chuckled. "This here's Jayne Kennedy. She ain't too bad."

"I guess I'll take it," Sebastian said, casually.

In the skating-rink parking lot, Sebastian selected the Bo Derek issue from the pile of *Playboy*s collecting on the backseat. Fizz sat in the car applying makeup while her brother stretched out on the hood of his car with the *Playboy* blocking his face. Stars began to settle in the sky like silver glitter against smoky gray paper. Teenagers sat inside opened car trunks smoking weed and drinking malt liquor from wrinkled paper bags. Some girls passed Sebastian and giggled.

"Empty heads," he called out behind them.

"Can we go in now?" I asked.

Changing the subject, Sebastian started a conversation about the article he was reading, called "Fast Times at Ridgemont High." "Man, kids are wild on the West Coast," he said, directing a smile toward us (his sister had recently resurfaced with pink-and-burgundy eyelids). Then he passed the magazine to us, joking, "Since you're both a little dense, you should read the part about the banana."

"What?" Fizz asked, confused.

"Clod," Sebastian retorted.

While my body grew warm from the story of a high school girl's first time, I leafed through the *Playboy* and imagined myself one of the naked women bent over as though looking for something underneath a bed. Just then a boy I'd known all my life walked by, and I saw him in a whole new light.

I caught a glimpse of Jason passing through the glimmering light poles illuminating the parking lot. I was able to follow the faint glow of his thin white T-shirt as he mingled with the rink crowd—the pack of teenage boys who wore their blue jean cuffs tucked under and carried in their back pockets those rough hand towels that came in packs of ten for a dollar. I hadn't seen him much that summer. He was hanging with a group of guys from the Cooper Road, the area bordering the city's sewage system.

Just then Sebastian turned to us and thankfully said, "Let's move in." Inside, we stood in the doorway waiting for our eyes to adjust to the darkness that sparked with tiny flicks of color from a disco ball floating in the middle of the room. The smell of oiled metal wheels mixed with marijuana overwhelmed me.

Sebastian folded his arms across his chest and raised his head only slightly when Ruby, who'd come with her own group of friends, greeted him. She, of course, ignored her immature niece. Behind her a couple of boys in double-breasted shirts stared at Fizz, a stream of fluorescent light peering through her bowlegs. We were twelve, the age in which either the female face takes on seductive angles or, as in my case, all hell breaks loose. To start with, I was of mean appearance. Each additional pimple tilted the scale less in my favor. While Fizz glowed like Brooke Shields being presented to her suitors in *Pretty Baby,* my hair had not yet recovered from the chemical scalping I'd endured years earlier. As we walked the parameters of the rink, admiring new dance routines and overhearing flattering comments about Fizz, vanity overpowered friendship and inwardly I found solace in the dim-wittedness of my friend.

Toward the back of the room I saw Jason again. This time he'd spotted me too and, out of character, skated my way.

"Hi," I said breathlessly. He smiled and sucked on his bottom lip.

"You been looking for me?" he asked grinning.

"What? I work for the police?" I laughed, but stopped when Jason pinned me against the wall. I hadn't been that close to him since grade school. Some things about him—the chipped front tooth, the disheveled hair, and the pointy ears—were the same. I didn't much care for the new features that complemented his roguish lifestyle—the deep furrow carved into his forehead and the tobacco-stained lips. Still, I felt damp all over.

Jason wobbled a bit on his skates, then pulled me into him. He placed his lips solidly atop mine, allowing his tongue to linger in my mouth until he felt he had succeeded in giving me my first kiss. I didn't like the bitter taste of the sweet-smelling peach schnapps he'd been drinking. Then he took from his faded pocket a silver clip that had a string of feathers hanging from it.

"It's a roach clip," he said, trying to sound like an authority.

I'd seen them before. Many people wore them as a fashion accessory, clipped in the hair or on the belt loop of a pair of jeans. For Jason, the clip served another purpose. Taking a twisted piece of paper he'd been smoking and clamping the clip's teeth around it, he inhaled deeply, and the paper all but disappeared.

Holding it out to me, he said, "Go ahead, baby." I thought about it. After all, what was the big deal? But I was saved, and saved people didn't do that. I shook my head.

"Whatever," he said, shrugging and turning his gaze on Fizz's flashing eyes. He asked her softly, "You want some?" To my utter amazement, Fizz took a long drag.

Still smiling at her, Jason skated off, mouthing, "I'll be back." His shadow disappeared into the darkness.

Finally, I thought to myself as Jason skated off. Finally, Fizz had done something to warrant the jealousy and rage that sometimes crept up inside me when I saw her. Now I could explain to Deacon Gardner why I didn't want to invite Fizz to church. Up until that puff she'd shared with Jason, I had no reason other than to say she had looks and independence, so she had enough. She didn't need salvation too.

The next Sunday I told Deacon Gardner and the class what had transpired at the rink, leaving out the underage drinking and replacing dope with cigarettes. During my passionate narrative of Fizz's betrayal, Deacon Gardner listened and nodded. When I had finished, a crooked smile crossed his face. "Let's see, Yolanda," he said, slowly removing his hand from the inside of his jacket pocket, "which one of those three I warned you about last week had ensnared your friend Fizz? Was it lust of the flesh?"

I twisted my head a little to glean the response of the rest of the class. Shel stared out in cockeyed contemplation and Tammy shook her head at me disapprovingly. It was Ruby who chimed in loudly, "Yolanda's the one who wanted Jason. She's the one lusting, Deacon Gardner."

I jerked my head over toward my accuser, but it was too late to say anything. Deacon Gardner had moved on.

"What about lust of the eye?" he asked in a hopeful tone. "Shel, what do you think?"

After taking a moment to straighten out his eyes, the deacon's son opened his mouth. At first nothing came out, but once something did I wished he'd kept his mouth shut.

"Well, Dad, last week you said that lust of the eye was like coveting something that someone else has, like being jealous of someone else's stuff, right?"

"Right," Deacon Gardner offered gleefully, sensing that his son was on the right track.

"Well, if that's the case, Yolanda is the one always talking about Fizz's hair and Fizz's brother and how Fizz can do anything she wants. It seems like Yolanda is jealous of Fizz."

I smacked my lips open and shot Shel a look of total disbelief.

"What do you have to say about that?" Deacon Gardner asked me.

"Nothing, I guess" was all I could muster.

"Well, then, it must be pride of life that tripped Fizz up." Before he could finish, hands flared up all around me. Even the silly boys who never listened couldn't wait to put their two cents in. Deacon Gardner ignored them and looked down to give me the opportunity to redeem myself. "What do you think, Yolanda?"

"I think," I stammered, suddenly realizing that my eyes were burning, "Fizz made me look like a fool in front of Jason. She hurt my pride." Boy, did the tears rain down against a row of snickers.

"Stop it," Deacon Gardner commanded the boys. "Stop it right now. We don't laugh at one another in this class. We embrace one another. We learn from each other's mistakes." Deacon Gardner, the embodiment of all things decent, lifted from his suit jacket a white handkerchief folded in squares and handed it to me but brought no further attention to my crying. He took a seat on the pew at the front of the room and turned to face us. "You see, class, we have Yolanda to thank for pointing out something very important." We all looked him over suspiciously, doubting he could really spin this one. "Last Sunday I began our discussion by asking you a question. Does anyone remember what it was?"

Shel felt he was on a roll, so he blurted out, "You asked us what it was that caused us to leave the light and go into the darkness?"

"Right, son," Deacon Gardner said proudly. Then he added, almost whispering, "Do you see how easy it is? It's like growing a garden. I plant the seeds, I water the grass and rake the leaves, but still weeds grow up. I pull them up as fast as I can, but I can never get them all. The best I can do is be mindful of how easy it is for them to get my flowers caught up." Deacon Gardner rubbed my shoulders solemnly, then prayed the benediction of watchfulness. Again, a shadow fell over the church, but there was no rush to get outside.

Cold Spell

> Do not forsake your mother's teachings. They will be a garland
> to grace your head and a chain to adorn your neck.
>
> *—Proverbs 1:19*

Our Southern city was experiencing a cold spell. Hail the size of pecans had pummeled our roof the night before, and snow was expected to pack the streets by late morning. Lying still in my bed, I hoped such a drastic shift in weather patterns would inspire Momma to deviate from her routine, but at the requisite time she appeared at my door in one of her Hawaiian-print dusters.

"Rise, Yolanda," she said, switching my ceiling-fan light on and off. I glared at her in a useless attempt to shake her resolve, but I couldn't ruffle Momma. The woman was steady, even-tempered, and thick-skinned (seven brothers and two failed marriages will do that to a person). That morning she was also determined to see me out of bed.

Shreveport winters were sneaky, but hardly ever icy. Usually an all-weather coat was sufficient for the season, but maybe twice in a decade cold would grab us by the throat. It would creep into our houses through cracks in the wooden walls and floor; outside, it caused elderly ladies to slip on frozen morning dew. Now it was exploiting the wedge growing between Momma and me. When all I wanted was to lie in bed under a mountain of quilts and sip hot lemon toddy, Momma would deny me such liberties, insisting, "School's your job, kid."

It was a waste of time trying to persuade her to my position. The only thing I'd ever seen her mind change about was a hair-style, and even that was more of an evolution. When I was a toddler, Momma had worn her hair in a pageboy bob. Throughout my grade-school years it was brushed back, pinned and crowned with the kind of hairpiece favored by Barbara Eden on *I Dream of Jeannie*. In truth Momma wore that style for a few seasons too long, but finally she settled on the convenience of her current do—a feathered coif, shagged in back and easily maintained with the bump of a curling iron.

By the time I was in junior high, Momma's busy schedule didn't allow much time to primp. Whether she'd fallen asleep watching a late-night Los Angeles Lakers home game or been nagged all night by a stuffy nose, when her alarm clamored at five-fifteen, Momma was up. In the quiet, she would read a few Scriptures and say her prayers. Then she would shower, make breakfast, and send me off before heading out with my baby brother.

Although the fire was churning in our central heating system, I felt the cold in my bones as soon as I pulled the sheets off. I draped the covers over my shoulders and walked over to my bedroom window. Frost coated the metal fence outside, and it seemed to me that everything was still asleep. Cedars had turned auburn, and thin pines bent over from the weight of icicles to form crystal gazebos. Every few minutes a glaciered tree branch snapped and shattered like glass.

I slipped into my robe and crossed the hall to the small bathroom I shared with my brother. I woke in the shower, then scrubbed my face with the Phisoderm Momma bought to combat my acne. After brushing my teeth with toothpaste and then baking soda, I went back into my bedroom to dress. A year earlier twin beds had been replaced by an antique white seven-piece bedroom suite—double bed, night tables, six-drawer bureau, desk, chair, and bookcase hutch—all provided by Momma's Bell South ransom. Her escape from the poverty pit had happened gradually and naturally, and I'd hardly taken notice. She'd held on to that first job just as she had the savings account she'd opened on a third-grade field trip to First National Bank. Like those cedar birds that used the same sweet-smelling evergreen twigs to rebuild nests year after year, Momma stuck with anything she found useful. With that job and savings account, Momma had bought the nicest house on our dour street and wheeled along in a number of used cars. (The Impala had survived a slipping transmission, several flat tires, and a small engine fire before finally giving out three years earlier.) Still, it vexed me that there was always money for the two-hundred-fifty-dollar emergency transmission repair but never enough for me to put another quarter into the Pac-Man arcade. Momma did, however, allow herself one indulgence—a new pair of Nina sandals at the end of every month. I suppose you could say that Momma was more judicious when it came to parting with a dollar than I was about leaving the house on cold winter mornings. Unfortunately, she controlled both.

Not only was I never late for school, but I'd never missed a full day of classes. I imagine that if I'd ever thrown up blood, fainted from a high fever, or experienced uncontrollable chills, Momma would have allowed me to stay home. I recall waking one morning with a crook in my neck; Momma simply wrestled me to the floor in order to pop my neck back into place. When I was sent home with pinkeye, Momma used Big Momma's prescription for eye cleansing—a few drops of my own pee, which ran down my cheek onto my lip and left in my mouth the taste of brine. I woke the next morning with eyes flushed of all redness and was promptly sent back to school.

I don't mean to imply that Momma was some cross between Lana Turner and Aunt Jemima, ever ridiculing while she toiled away in the kitchen. She was as capable as the next thirty-one-year-old of a little playful whimsy: Bobby Womack played on her radio and Danielle Steel books lay across her bed. She owned an impressive collection of clutch purses, and for a while she carried in them Salem 100s.

In the kitchen that cold morning, the usual salmon croquettes, eggs, and biscuits waited in the warm oven. I sat at the table slowly smearing fig preserves on a hot biscuit while Momma rushed from room to room tidying stacks of papers, clearing counters, and matching a purse to her shoes, while a nagging voice assured me that I was nothing like my mother. While she was single-minded, I vacillated on every topic, except my hair. After what became known as "the perm fiasco," I did everything possible to avoid altering it—I wore beaded braids in the summer and in the winter a stiff set of pineapple waves. In the area of competency, a few unfortunate incidents— losing my house keys, then unwisely deciding to enter through a window; washing my colors and whites in hot water all at once; and twice dropping my baby brother on the kitchen floor—had proved that I was not my mother's daughter. There was also the problem of my spendthrift ways—my weekly seven-dollar allowance collected every Friday was gone before Monday. And while Momma was disciplined and dedicated, I could sometimes be lax; on a day when the temperature was below freezing I thought it reasonable to stay home from school.

To make matters worse, that year Momma was scheduled to work a split shift three days a week, which meant she would work from nine-thirty A.M. until two, come home for a late lunch, then go back to work from five until nine-thirty. I hated Momma's split-shift days as much as I hated the days when my breath froze, because both required more of me. With Momma working, I'd have to make sure my brother ate the dinner Momma left for us, wash and stack our dishes, vacuum the carpet, and perform any other unsavory chores Momma had outlined for me. But I never did the job well enough and would have to listen to Momma gripe. Once I tried to guilt-trip her with a wisecrack about not asking to be born. That woman just turned her lips up in annoyance and shouted back at me, "I don't see you trying to make a quick exit," punctuating her statement with a finger thump on my forehead.

I was thinking about those battles when Momma noticed me picking at my salmon croquettes. "Why are you still here?" she asked, knowing that I was hoping for a reprieve from school. "I'm not taking you to school if you miss that bus after lazing around."

I pushed my feet, padded with three pairs of socks, into my cowboy boots, pulled on my turquoise ski cap and matching wool gloves, and buttoned up my coat, which was warm but long past its fashion moment. I ventured out into the wintry air. My teary eyelashes grew cold on my face.

I was the last to arrive at the bus stop, where the gas station manager had mercifully invited everyone into his little booth to wait amidst the cans of motor oil. After about fifteen minutes had passed, I announced to the others, "I'm going back home." They advised me against this. Over the years many of them had become acquainted with Momma's wrath. I went back anyway.

It was around seven-thirty when I opened the front door and heard the "cha-clink, cha-clink, cha-clink." Momma sat in front of her old typewriter, stiffly pressing its keys, making a sound like coins being tossed into a pile.

"What are you doing?" I asked, bristling at the cold coming in behind me.

"Taking my own advice," she said. A clerk-typist position in the company's sales office had come open, she told me, but she needed to be able to type seventy words per minute. The job meant straight business working hours, holidays and week-ends off.

"When's the last time you typed, Momma?" I asked her.

"Years, baby, years, but I've got two weeks to get back up to speed."

I must have looked odd standing in that doorway just staring at Momma fidgeting with papers, banging on stiff keys, before finally lowering her head in frustration and saying, "We'll see." Only then did she realize I wasn't supposed to be there and asked what I was doing back home. I said that I'd forgotten a book and quickly rushed back out of the house, my boots crunching the frozen grass as I crossed our front lawn.

When I returned to the gas station, the bus had come and gone. Going back home was not an option. For once I was going to do what the situation required. The way Momma always did. It was easy to take her for granted, the way I took for granted that the sun would overtake the cold on winter mornings.

Our house was always filled with the sounds of her hands busying themselves, with dishes, flowerpots, scissors. And smells—on her off days she was scented with Pine Sol and Lemon Pledge. On Sundays it was Estée Lauder perfume. Then there were the things she baked—rosemary chicken, cheese-and-broccoli casseroles, and an assortment of fruity cakes. The refrigerator was always stacked with Tupperware containers, the fruit compartment filled with pears and canteloupe, the vegetable tray stuffed with greens. Copper pots and cake molds hung from freshly painted cream walls. Mitts and dish towels were folded neatly in a drawer underneath the sink. The medicine cabinet was always stocked with extra toothbrushes, Band-Aids, and a bitter yellow bottle of 666. Boxes in the washroom stored special platters and tablecloths for the Fourth of July, Thanksgiving, and Christmas.

On the few days when Momma was unable to keep up with the pace she'd set, I resented her. It took a cold day and a bus mishap for me to come to understand that Momma needed my help, and I vowed to be a burden no longer. When at the city bus stop a trash collector told me that I'd just missed the bus and at the rate they were moving another one wouldn't be around for an hour, I decided to walk the three miles to school.

First I climbed the levee that cradled the highway. I walked down Youree Drive and passed the Southern Maid Donut Shop, breathing in the smell of frying sugar dough and coffee that broke through the frigid air. I decided to stop and have a donut and some hot chocolate. The warm pastry melted like cotton candy in my mouth. The cocoa warmed my hands and face enough for me to go on. Sometime that morning I thought of Momma, who in her own way walked alone in the cold. One of the drawbacks to life as a single mother seemed to be isolation.

The woman seldom went out on dates or got to goof off with her brothers at their weekend baseball games—not because she didn't want to but because she was just plain busy.

Even though motherhood had come early, Momma managed as though she had always been prepared. As I thought about it I realized that there had been missteps—the charred pot of string beans that resulted from Momma's absorption in a book, as well as the makeshift hole in my leotard that was often necessary because she never remembered my size. When my mother's skills did not come naturally, she worked harder, and good things, like a better job, happened.

The snow the weatherman had predicted began to fall in clumps like cotton balls as I passed the looming shadow of Broadmoor Baptist Church. I remember walking the last few blocks to school wondering what it would take for me to be more like my mother after all. I arrived at class in time to sign my tardy slip and be erased from the first-period absentee list. Before I could remove my coat, the announcement I'd been hoping for came over the intercom.

"Line up," Mr. Heard bellowed. "School has been dismissed."

Thirteen

Better to be nobody and yet have a servant than
to pretend to be somebody and have no food.

—Proverbs 12:9

In the mail on my thirteenth birthday, inside a crumpled business envelope between the folds of lined yellow paper, I found a letter from my father and a money order for five hundred dollars. The note was short, written in bird scratch, and promised that Jack would visit soon. Only my father would think that his slot-machine winnings could even the score for all the times he'd come up short on birthdays and Christmases. I was at an age when any excitement was greeted with a touch of ennui, and I was no longer willing to get all worked up like Charlie Brown every time Jack held out a football. So I placed my focus on the bird in hand, which in this case was a nice-size nest egg.

Momma had wanted to deposit the money into a five-year certificate that I could only withdraw for college. I argued against this. I was, after all, thirteen—to my mind three quarters of the way to adulthood but to Momma only halfway to having any sense. In addition to now being a teenager, I was also a student council officer, band flag girl, and Quiz Team star. And the esteem that had been showered on my friends at Stoner Hill only increased at our new school; Jason's roguish manner made him dead attractive to all the girls, as did Dwight's charm. Talkative Teresa had flipped her way onto the cheerleading squad. And Fizz was still beautiful. We outsiders had arrived at Broadmoor in outfits that mimicked the Soul Train dancers and *Ebony Magazine* models—dark colors like burgundy and purple, on heavy fabrics of polyester and suede. The kids on the inside wore light pastels, even in the winter. Gradually, the black kids started to change in order to fit in. It was also early in the Reagan era, and everybody wanted to look like they had money. By the time our eighth-grade year began, we had resolved to be preppy.

The boys from Stoner Hill wore faded-out baby blue oxford shirts and imitation Bass Weejun loafers. Some even took to carrying monogrammed attaché cases. Dwight, whose grandparents were still giving him whatever he wanted, was the only black boy capable of wearing originals consistently. He alone smelled of Polo cologne and carried crisp dollar bills in a velcro Izod wallet. When space in his small closet ran out, my friend took to hanging his madras and solid-colored shirts like national flags from an exposed ceiling pipe in his room.

Growing up, I remember old people in our neighborhood saying, "Child, you better cover yourself." Depending on the circumstances, the expression usually had one of two meanings. Either a teen was dressed revealingly and actually needed to put on more clothes, or someone had made an error in judgment and needed to explain themselves. The phrase could also be a way to describe what the kids from Stoner Hill were trying to do—cover up who we were. We were trying to be somebody else.

Even Jason, whose family's electricity was cut off more often than it was turned on, was not immune. Weed and failing grades may have been turning him into an NTB, a no-talent bum, but he too was a preppy wannabe. He'd convinced the owner of one of those buffet steak houses to pay him three dollars an hour to bus tables and wash dishes thirty hours a week. Every Saturday morning after picking up his paycheck, he and Dwight would take the bus to the mall. When he caught a sale, he could purchase several items at once, say, a shirt with a crest over the chest pocket, a pair of jeans, and maybe some matching socks. Other times, out of sheer necessity, he would be forced to blow his whole salary on one "must-have"—a down-stuffed vest or a pair of L. L. Bean Maine hunting shoes. After a spree there might not be money left for the bus ride home. That didn't matter. He would walk to work, so long as it meant he could buy more camouflage at the end of the week. Once when Jason didn't have enough money to buy a new shirt to wear to the state fair, he lifted a crisp white button-down from its hanger, stuffed it under his shirt, and quickly walked out of the store.

I empathized with Jason because I was also living a double life—the one I wanted and the one I had. Over the summer I accidentally befriended Kimberly Wrye, the white girl who had also been elected to the student council. Without much fuss, our conversations shifted from deciding who'd read the morning announcements over the P.A. system to who was the most attractive among the boys. Still, I never showed Kimberly all of who I was, the Yolanda my friends from Stoner Hill knew.

Phone call to Kimberly:

Me: My dad sent me five hundred dollars for my birthday, and he promised to come visit before the school year ends.

Kimberly: Maybe I can meet him. Where does he live?

Me: All over. He docks around the bay in Galveston?

Kimberly: Your dad has a boat. I didn't know you sailed.

Me: I'm hoping my dad can teach me.

And the Yolanda of Stoner Hills . . . phone call to Fizz:

Me: Got a letter from that no-good daddy of mine today.

Fizz: Anything in it?

Me: Five hundred bones.

Fizz: Cool. Where's he at?

Me: I don't know. He says he's moved to the Gulf, but the postage was from Dallas.

Fizz: Niggas will lie, won't they?

For my birthday Kimberly bought me my own copy of *The Official Preppy Handbook*, explaining she had grown leery of loaning out hers—a favor often solicited since she was considered the KPOC (Key Prep on Campus). In short, I, with a frizzy perm, a clumsy build, and a propensity for canker sores, had somehow managed to become, in the most immature and clichéd manifestation, popular.

Since it is generally known that most thirteen-year-olds suffer from lunacy, I do not cower when acknowledging that *The Preppy Handbook* was my bible. I wanted to look, walk, and talk like a certain kind of student who sat in a particular place in the cafeteria, and I adjusted my speech to include their preppy lexicon, a vocabulary hinged on pure irony. To suggest that something was "nice" meant that it was the farthest thing from; a student with a "good attitude" was quite the jerk; a "classic" referred to someone with strange tendencies; and "tapioca" had nothing to do with food but instead implied that you were flat broke. The mission of the in crowd (of which I considered myself a vital part) was to hoist ourselves above all the NTB's.

Momma didn't care for any of this. I explained I was only imitating the handbook's air—innocent sarcasm mixed with a contrived worldliness. Almost everything that I uttered—"suuure," "wooonderful," "good for you"—was accompanied by an exaggerated gesture, like rolling my eyes to the back of my head.

How was I to know that the book was meant to mock rather than instruct? The advice it offered may have been a joke to its authors, but it became my ideal. "A trivial and fruitless pursuit," Momma warned. I wondered aloud if she even remembered being thirteen. For the first time since I'd arrived at Broadmoor, I didn't feel like an outsider, dumbfounded by the punch line of every joke, staring down at my shoes for fear that the eyes I met would turn away. Being an insider seemed worth sacrificing the real me; if I was less recognizable to myself, I was known by others, and there was a certain kind of joy in that.

Being preppy wasn't just about being popular and talking the talk, I explained to Momma. I also needed to walk the walk the way my white friend Kimberly and her family did. My neighbor Timmy Phipps and I had caught the bus to Kimberly's house for student council planning meetings the previous summer. Without fail, Kimberly would greet us at the door looking like the preppy drawing diagrammed in the handbook—a grosgrain ribbon twisted around her hair, pearls accenting her earlobes and neck, a soft cotton sweater either draped over her slightly wrinkled Lacoste shirt or hugging her Bermuda shorts. Inside the house, ducks were stitched on everything from the sofa cushions to Kimberly's watchband. Two beaks propped books together, and an entire flock swam across Mrs. Wrye's dress as she poured herself another glass of wine. There seemed a great deal to toast.

The family had finally graduated to the Big House, replete with a pool in the backyard. Mrs. Wrye didn't have a particular affinity for ducks or the pool, but she felt it was worth mentioning to Kimberly's junior high school friends that these things were "in."

I listened up and coveted everything in Kimberly's home. Timmy, on the other hand, didn't care about anything but the Wryes' aquarium-shaped pool. He had risen to the level of Shark at the Y and could do anything in a swimming pool— dive, butterfly, backstroke—only our community pool was crowded with amateurs all summer long.

On the bus ride home from Kimberly's one afternoon, Timmy turned to me and declared, "I'm going to get a pool like that one day."

"Suuure you are, Timmy," I said sarcastically, then was quieted by his stony gaze. We rode the rest of the way in silence.

While most Stoner Hill moms would have smacked Timmy simply for allowing himself such pie-in-the-sky delusions, Timmy's mom took him around the city pricing houses with pools and got inspired herself. She leaned over to her son, smiled hopefully, and said, "We might be able to do this."

The opportunity was due to her job as a car-door painter for General Motors. The plant was like a human forklift that hoisted penniless people up and out of poor neighborhoods like Stoner Hill. Some, like Timmy's mom, chose to stay in the neighborhood, opting instead for a brand-new Cadillac, which in GM's upscale parking lot was about as hard to find as a tuber in a five-pound bag of potatoes.

"We'll have to sacrifice," Timmy's mom told him, then

demonstrated what she meant by selling her white Seville. With the proceeds she started a new-house savings account. A succession of desists followed. For one whole year Timmy and his younger sister had to endure life without Pizza Hut, Taco Bell, or even an occasional Happy Meal from McDonald's. They saw not a single movie that school year and survived without cable TV. And the thing that was just beyond "nice" was that Mrs. Phipps wouldn't buy them any new clothes.

Timmy had readily agreed to all of this. Unfortunately, he'd also grown three inches over the summer, while his pants hem only extended two. As we boarded the school bus on the first day of eighth grade, Timmy, thanks to his high-waters (sooo *très déclassé*), was met with a stream of indignities: "You're flooding"; "High Water Timmy"; and the like. Not the least of which came from Jason, who'd always thought of Timmy as a good-attitude student. I joined in, shouting, "Nice pants," to get Timmy to move away from me.

By my estimation, Timmy had committed the ultimate faux pas. I could see no social return for him. Black people prided themselves on having style. What clothes lacked in quality, they made up for in flamboyance of cut and color—bright reds and yellows, wide lapels, and chunky shoes. Big Momma would prefer to drop dead in the street rather than walk into church without a hat on. No surprise, it took a black person to figure out that smooth tar and spit could really shine a pair of dull black shoes. For our parents' generation, the clothes had just been about looking good, but now we wanted to look not just good but good like somebody else. Timmy reminded me of what I was trying so hard to get away from.

"Let me get this straight," Momma challenged during our continuing debate over what to do with my money, a hand on her right hip, her head cocked to the left. "You don't have a pot to piss in or a window to throw it out, but you want to put a forty-two-dollar shirt on your back?"

"It's one hundred percent cotton," I stressed.

"Who raised you, child?" Momma asked, worn down. For the entirety of her existence my momma had lived in the same neighborhood, prayed in the same church, and studied in the same school. Let her walk in my shoes and have to spend her days with people who made assumptions about her and, worse yet, assumptions that were true: that I had no decent father and that money sometimes ran low. Had she really wanted to know, it was not *who* was raising me, but what I was being raised on, and I could have told her *The Facts of Life* and *Diff'rent Strokes.* I wanted to be a preppy, with a nickname like Buffy, and with rich people's problems, like whether to hook my leather belt with whales or lobsters. I wanted to be one of those white people lounging in the grass outside the country club with a little horse and jockey on my chest.

Momma finally threw up her hands in exasperation and, against her better judgment, agreed to let me spend every last dime of my bounty on a TDC (total design concept). So a few days after I'd eaten the last of my Halloween candy, I stood next to a pile of leaves armed with my five hundred dollars, waiting for the bus to take me on my first real shopping spree.

Pope's Clothier was a preppy hybrid of Brooks Brothers, J. Press, and Abercrombie & Fitch. It had the rustic charm of a converted horse stable and the riding motif to carry it off. With its three-hundred-dollar sterling silver liquor flasks and rows of Gucci purses, it catered to Shreveport's affluent country club community. Stepping onto the store's quiet and cushy carpet, I was surrounded by strawberry and apple print dresses, embroidered sweaters, and leather Pappagallo Blossoms. It was a beautiful thing but also a little intimidating. I was happy the handbook had provided me with detailed instructions on how to deal with a salesperson. There was really nothing left for me to do but make a fool of myself.

A waif of a saleslady approached, appearing confused by my presence in the store. "May I help you?" she asked.

I followed rule number one and spoke politely but with authority. I blurted out the words "darling" and "divine" in a trifling attempt to sound as if I belonged, which was unnecessary because all the saleslady cared about was my cash, and she helped me spend it all. Five hundred dollars didn't stretch like I thought it would, but I managed to come away with three Shetland sweaters, five Ralph Lauren cotton button-downs (three plaid, two solid), thick Polo socks in every color, a pair of heavy khakis, and kelly green cords.

In truth, my Polo shirts held their crease long after ironings and felt soft against my skin, but I had been prepared to wear them even if they'd scratched my behind like a burlap sack. I had not learned how to properly care for my clothes, and by year's end my shirttails were tattered with wear and all my pants had shrunk and faded as a result of my hot-water washes. The only designer item I owned that still looked good was my Coach purse—a ten-year-old hand-me-down from the lady Honeymoon worked for. Momma said that most of my outfits wouldn't be wearable next year, so in the fall I'd have to reacquaint myself with the clothes she could afford to buy me. I had blown five hundred dollars in one day and, unlike my old friend Timmy, had nothing to show for it.

During Mardi Gras break that year I was with the other neighborhood kids playing volleyball in the street when a big

U-Haul truck backed into Timmy's front yard. I watched as some friends of his mom's carried chairs, mattresses, and boxes of clothes and dishes from the house out onto the truck. I marched up to Timmy's front door, half amazed and half mad, and demanded to know what in the world was going on.

"I told you, Momma said we could get a house with a pool if we could sacrifice for a little while," Timmy reminded me while blocking my entry into his former home. "Oh, that's right," he added wryly. "You didn't believe."

Timmy, in his cut-off khakis, worn Top-Siders, and sleeveless Polo shirt, resembled a cuter version of the Incredible Hulk, but it had taken me too long to see his appeal.

"So you're leaving?" I asked. "Now? What about school?"

"They've got better ones across town." He may as well have shouted, "In your eye" to me. I realized then that Timmy had more than any of us, even before his mom bought the big house. He had a vision and was willing to pursue it even if doing so made him a target of jokes. I should have told him to go for it, that getting your own pool is an excellent idea, but I was too busy pretending to be instead of becoming. Before I could gather myself to apologize to Timmy, he blew me off. "I'll catch you later," he said. "We're about to bolt." Then he closed the door in my face.

Once again, Momma's infinite wisdom had proven right. "It doesn't make sense to pay that kind of money for clothes and not have anything left in your pocket. Don't try to dress like you've arrived until you do," she'd advised me one last time as I left for my shopping spree. The novelty of being "in" was short-lived, especially after I discovered that being in didn't make you equal. Kimberly had commented on the decline in my attire, and I didn't much feel like her friend anymore.

I sat in my driveway watching Timmy help empty out his little house and imagined what it would be like for him living in a neighborhood like Kimberly's with a pool right there in his backyard. The truck pulled off just before a sheet of black fell over the day. I went into my bedroom and decided to reread my *Preppy Handbook* in the hope that it would cheer me up. At the end of the book I ran across a passage I'd never paid any attention to before. It seemed that the word "preppy" had been coined in the novel *Love Story*, wherein the narrator muses, "Just what is a Preppy? A guy who dresses perfectly without trying to. He appears to do everything well with ease."

When the handbook asked the novel's author, Erich Segal, for the etymology of the word, he, a classics scholar, replied in facetious irony, "It's a derivative of the word 'preposterous.'" I thought that just about summed up my whole year.

Can We Be Healed?

Heal me, O Lord, and I will be healed, save me and
I will be saved, for you are the one I praise.

—Jeremiah 17:14

Big Momma's hands lay almost lifeless on a quilt sewn with her
own knuckled fingers years earlier when her hands were as
strong as bird's feet. The cover's construction contradicted all
the rules of quilt making. Its pieces, scraps really, were seldom
100 percent cotton. Big Momma would use silk, wool, and, most
often, some blend of polyester. Instead of hand stitching, she'd
embroidered the blanket using her sewing machine. She hadn't
wasted time laying the cut squares out in a pattern beforehand.
Instead, she'd just pulled scraps haphazardly from a bag and
allowed fate to determine its design as she went along. All winter long, between Sunday suppers, family uproar, and community crises, Big Momma would spin out quilts. Then the spring
would come and pruning season would begin. Only that spring
Big Momma had gotten so sick I doubted she had the strength
to twist the top off one of her mason jars.

As the cool settled in on that warm evening, neighbors and church people gathered outside Big Momma's window praying and singing hymns, as if time had turned back to the days when slaves would sneak out to worship in hush harbors, the spots where swamps met the edge of cotton fields.

The family stirred inside Big Momma's four-room block-house, taking in the memories of pine-scented quilts, morning doses of cod liver oil, and hearty meals of dumplings, whole okra, and hens. By her hands we'd been warmed, nourished, and cured. Now we hoped our healing ceremony would do the same for her. Already Big Momma had taken on the look of a dead woman—sunken-in eyes, swollen joints, thin, lifeless hair. Her nails were cracking, and her skin was so dry that scaly seams ran up her legs.

Big Momma's affliction had been a slow process, taking her energy bit by bit. Sugar diabetes had attacked her body gradually. Eventually, all Big Momma could do was lie still, too tired to even roll over for a change of sheets.

People had different ways of getting through the deathwatch, though we all avoided eye contact. Big Momma's oldest son, Peter, spent most of his time on Big Momma's front porch, inhaling Salems and digging his hands deeply into his front pockets, one fist clinching the cellophane-wrapped cigarettes, the other clasping the cold, scuffed silver lighter. Honeymoon acted as a nursemaid, dipping and wringing towels to place on Big Momma's head, seeing to her comfort by adjusting her legs, back, and bedsheets, monitoring her bowel movements and breathing regularity.

In the kitchen were Big Momma's sisters, Piggy and Mary—younger by a few years but still very old—who busied themselves by kneading dough for biscuits, pie shells, dumplings, and whatever else they could imagine, while ignoring their own swells of sickness.

If Big Momma died, I feared our family would drift apart, lost like our quilt-making tradition. She alone followed the process from start to end—never complaining of the needle punctures and back strain. Everyone else saw only bits and pieces of the endeavor—the material scraps randomly laid out over the floor, and later those same scraps sewn in a colorful pattern and folded on top of her bed. Then for Christmas, a birthday, or sometimes for no reason at all, she'd cover us with a warm, vibrant blanket. Big Momma always tried to protect us from the suffering that went along with things. Maybe that's why we didn't realize how sick she was until she just couldn't sit up any longer.

My great-grandmother was not the only one among us who needed to be healed. Some of our afflictions seemed small, like my wondering when my hair would grow back. Others were more serious, like Uncle Peter's raspy cough, and Honeymoon and Pappy's worries about money. As we sat together in Big Momma's living room, you could almost hear hearts breaking— Baby Jane's marriage was in trouble.

Before she got sick, Big Momma's age—she was nearing eighty then—did not deter any one of us from piling onto her chest one idle concern after another. Even with her failing health, she was usually able to give us some relief from our problems, either by solving them or by reminding us that "everybody's got a cross." I could crawl onto her bed, lay my head below her chin, and she'd calm me saying, "Now, if the son of God had to suffer slander, betrayal, and ultimately murder, Lord have mercy on what's bound to come to us."

I thought of that frequent quotation as I watched Big

Momma's two preaching children prepare to begin the healing service. For years her daughter Doll had worked at the hospital, changing bedpans and bathing newborn babies. She had prayed over them for free. She said that God spoke to her one sunrise and told her to go out and preach his word. She sewed herself a crimson robe, bought an old trailer, and sat it in her front yard with a posterboard sign that read, FAITH TEMPLE. Inside the narrow quarters—there were two pianos, a dozen plastic flower arrangements, and an assortment of grocery bags stuffed with books and clothes—Aunt Doll's members multiplied, because it was said that she could lay hands on the ailing and they would be healed.

"All right now, gather round, y'all." Aunt Doll led us into a prayer circle in the living room, where leaking white candles emitted the smell of hot wax.

"Lord, precious Jesus, Holy One," she began her prayer, "heal us today." Afterward she bowed her head toward me, saying, "Young one, read."

I began:

Be merciful to me, Lord, for I am faint; heal me, for my bones are in agony. . . . My soul is in anguish. . . . I am worn out from groaning; all night long I flood my bed with weeping and drench my couch with tears. My eyes grow weak with sorrow; they fail because of all my foes. . . . The Lord has heard my cry for mercy; and the Lord accepts my prayer.

As I read from the ink-stained pages, Big Momma's youngest son, Uncle Frazier, began singing the hymn "I Love the Lord, He Heard My Cry." The family and those outside joined in.

Following one behind the other, Aunt Doll, Honeymoon, and their brothers walked into their mother's adjacent bedroom, each manning a corner of her bed. Aunt Doll, standing at Big Momma's right, dipped two fingers into a glass of olive oil and rubbed them over Big Momma's brow. I watched this ceremony with the rest of the family who remained in the living room, humming and taking turns (from the youngest on up) reading from Big Momma's Bible.

Though the living room was the only sitting room in the house, people seldom got to lounge there, choosing the large kitchen or front porch instead. Since Big Momma fell sick, her prized antiques—the miniature black kettles with minstrel faces brushed on, the china plates with pictures of Scarlett O'Hara, and the hand-painted ceramic chickens—all collected dust. Her iron skillets, seasoned just so, hung cold from wall hooks, and even her garden grew wild and frantic.

I couldn't really feel it, but all these things cried out that soon Big Momma would be gone, leaving only her fingerprints—flower- and butterfly-embroidered sheets and pillowcases, the quilts stacked in padded layers on the beds, last season's pears, figs, and peaches sealed tightly in thick glass jars. Panic swelled up in me, and I broke from the circle and ran out the back door. I sat on the back steps listening to the healing revival and watching a spider spin a web in the corner of Big Momma's porch.

"What does it take to be healed?" I heard Aunt Doll holler from Big Momma's bedroom. I yearned to know.

Walking out into the yard, I pulled back the bare limbs of fruit trees, smelling the rot of the fallen ones. I crawled into the exposed doghouse. Big Momma's German shepherd had frozen to death the winter before when she had been hospitalized during a sleet storm. That's what happens to you when you're left out alone. You die.

When the thought came to me in that cedar doghouse, in the

loneliness of the dark, I cried hard and loud, and then I started talking. I gave up concerns for myself, and a thought came to me—I could talk straight to God. I had never done so before. I'd said my prayers every night before going to bed and over every meal I ate, but it had been with the same zeal as I said the Pledge of Allegiance every morning in school. I'd never doubted the truth in the words, but I'd never felt them either.

I was only thirteen years old and wasn't sure how to talk to God, so I made my initial request in a demanding way. "Heal Big Momma, heal Big Momma," I kept saying over and over again. Then my demands turned to pleas: "Lord, please heal Big Momma. Please, Lord." Then I began negotiations. "Lord, I promise I'll stop talking about people, and I'll stop talking back to Momma. I'll just do what she tells me to do."

This went on for a time, with the faint sound of singing in the air. When I got up, I went back into the house to see if Big Momma had been healed. Judging from the tired expressions on my family's faces and the sadness with which Honeymoon patted Big Momma's face down, it appeared that nothing had happened.

I sat down, quietly praying that God's will be done. Then a miracle happened. A blanket of peace fell over me, as gentle and familiar as the hand of Big Momma. And slowly she came back to us. The next morning she was able to breathe a little more freely. A while later she could talk softly. She said she needed air, so all the curtains and windows were opened. Finally, Big Momma asked, "Mary, fix me something to eat." I don't think it occurred to anyone else that day that sick people had been given the power to heal Big Momma and that this must have meant that we could heal ourselves.

Big Momma was never her same self again. She never

put her weight back on. She grew tired easily, and eventually she couldn't take care of herself and had to move in with Honeymoon, but she still hummed hymns, pulled me to her shoulders to whisper words of faith, and spread out her quilts of love.

Sometimes Angels Sing Off-Key

Because you are my help, I sing in the shadow of your wings.

—*Psalms 63:7*

One Sunday in late spring I was to sing a solo in the St. Peter Baptist Church youth choir. I wasn't nervous in the slightest because everyone there was family. The church was dominated by a few families that outsiders thought could be easily summed up: the Joneses, who thought themselves sophisticated but whom everyone else called stuck-up; the Montgomerys, who, all agreed, were a bunch of well-educated, hysterical fools; the Jacksons, all dark and somber; the Parkers, who were filled with emotion and lunacy; and us, a loud brood of working-class folks. But there was much more to us than that.

As a child, I was in church more days of the week than I was in school. My weekday evenings were filled with senior choir practice, teachers' meeting, prayer meeting, and Bible study; on Saturdays was youth-choir rehearsal. For over two hours impatient teens tolerated giggling grade-schoolers, and together our voices echoed over the empty pews. We would open with a tired devotional hymn, before rocking our shoulders to an up-tempo number that with a few lyric changes could play at the skating rink. No matter what slow tune we used to wind down, we always closed practice by singing our finale song, "They That Wait Upon the Lord."

By Sunday morning, after gargling with warm salt water, washing and pressing our choir robes, and praying for the intervention of harmony and the Holy Ghost, we were ready. From the moment the organist hit her first chord, the ladies in the pews stood on their feet, waved their hands, shouted Hallelujah, and sometimes jumped into a holy dance. The men leaned their heads forward and back murmuring, "Sing that, say that." If we really got them going, Miss Carrie sometimes grabbed her wig and flung it across the pulpit. Deacon Abrams, sitting with his white patent-leather lace-ups crossed over each other, would yelp something resembling a hiccup. As we swayed back and forth in unison, our eyes clouded with tears, our foreheads beaded with perspiration, and our hands and feet ached from our rhythmic claps and stomps. Our voices, the harp strings of angels, sent floating messages from God to the parishioners. Or so I thought.

The Sunday of my solo I formally asked Fizz and Teresa to come to church and hear our youth choir sing. They accepted the invitation in part to see if my choir lived up to all the bragging I'd done. While singing a solo verse of "Jesus Christ Is the Way," I smiled down at them. They didn't smile back. They sat with puzzled expressions, crossed eyes, and twisted lips. Teresa looked as though her head was about to spin off.

"You can't sing," they announced before we were out the church doors.

"Yes, I can," I murmured, already losing confidence.

"No, you can't," Teresa said. She pointed out further, "Your voice cracks when you try to hit the high notes, and the choir sings off-key."

I didn't want to believe them, but the next Sunday I didn't sing with the youth choir and sat with the congregation, claiming a sore throat but wanting to discover whether what my friends said was true. Moved to the edge of my pew, I listened to the sopranos stumble through the first stanza.

"They that wait upon the Lord shall renew their strength." Then the altos joined in: "They that wait upon the Lord shall renew their strength." Finally the tenors: "They that wait upon the Loorrdddd." I could hardly stay in my seat. They all sounded like choking frogs. My friends had been right. Even with all the strained neck muscles and bulging eyes, not a single note was delivered in tune.

I looked around at the congregation. The old ladies were waving their hands, and the men had their eyes closed and their heads thrown back, as if listening to God himself sing. I was ashamed of us all.

At home that night I cornered Momma. "Y'all a bunch of liars and hypocrites down at St. Peter," I said in the thick drawl I always took on when I got angry.

"What are you talking about?" Momma stopped mixing the corn bread batter and stared at me.

"Y'all up in the Lord's house pretending," I yelled. "Throwing your hands up, flinging your hats off, running around the pews and bumping into doors, talking about 'the children have the spirit,' when you can hear that we can't even sing." For proof and affect, I threw my hands in the air and my hair ribbon across the room the way Miss Carrie flung her wig.

"You better stop playing with God, Miss Yolanda."

"But that's what y'all do," I fired back.

"No, Yolanda. We shout because our children love God," Momma said softly. "And it seems that the more we encourage you, the better you sound. We're shouting about the potential we see in you." Momma turned her back to me, her elbows waving out to the rhythm of the batter whisk.

Around the same time, a renowned mezzo-soprano came to Shreveport. I was hopeful that hearing her would give me back my wings. Our choir director had told us about the singer's performances at Carnegie Hall and the Metropolitan Opera House in New York, and I couldn't wait to hear the beautiful voice that had come to our local Strand Theater to perform a series of spirituals and classic arias in a one-woman show.

The Strand had recently been converted from a movie house to a grand auditorium. The ceiling was etched in gold leaf and supported by giant pillars that stood on red velvet carpet. After the lights were dimmed, a veiled orchestra began to play. As the curtain rose, so too did a voice soft and high. "Swing low, sweet chariot . . ." For fear of missing a sound, I held my breath as she captured us with "Ave Maria" and "Sweet Li'l Jesus," and I prayed to sing just one note like that in all my life. For the rest of the performance the audience was at her feet, enraptured by this elegant black woman draped in satin. Her back was completely straight, and her shoulders only moved when she took in a breath. She looked to me like a heavenly seraph.

We waited backstage, eager to be blessed with the diva's signature on our programs. In front of me a girl of about fourteen flapped about almost hysterical with excitement.

"I'm in the choir at Magnet High," she said, turning to me. "I'm going to be a diva someday and sing at the Strand and even at the great opera houses in New York, Italy, and Paris." Finally, her turn came to approach the table.

"I love you," the girl squealed in our thick drawl.

"Um-hmmm," the singer replied without lifting a single feathered lash from the program she was signing.

"I want to be an opera singer just like you one day," the girl stammered, her confidence slipping. "I practice very hard in my classical music classes, and my teacher says that I may have a voice like yours one day."

The woman finished her autograph in a flourish of annoyance. "Really?" she asked, releasing a quiet laugh. And that was all.

The next Sunday I was back in the choir, back in the crowded little red-brick church where the worn floorboards and walls trembled from the vibrations of an organ that took up half the pulpit. As the musicians hunched over their instruments and the stage bounced from foot stomping, the choir began to sing. The sopranos came in with their usual scratchiness. "They that wait upon the Lord shall renew their streenngth." Then it was my turn, along with the rest of the altos. "They that wait upon the Lord shall renew their streenngth." I closed my eyes tight and listened not to the sound of the tenors but to the words of our song. Our voices scaled in faltering unison: "They that wait upon the Lord shall renew their streenngth. . . . THEY SHALL MOUNT UP ON WINGS LIKE AN EAGLE!"

After six long months of practicing the hymn, I finally understood the meaning behind the lyrics. Our singing needn't be perfect or even in key. All that our choir had to do was to wait patiently, to grow, to improve, strengthened by the shelter of the people who knew and loved us. In the shadow of their praises, I looked out and saw that from the saints in the prayer corner to the ushers at the back door, there was not a muffled voice or lowered hand, only praises, holy dances, and hallelujahs lifting us another octave, giving us flight. When I learned that some won't so much as throw a smile of encouragement our way, the tossing of an old woman's wig became an uplifting deed.

Momma's Bullet Rising

The sun of righteousness will rise with healing in its wings.

—*Malachi 4:2*

The week before Easter of my eighth-grade year, the bullet below Momma's butter-smooth skin rose to the surface. Ten years earlier, at the time of Jack's assault, the doctors had decided not to remove it. Since then the slug had snailed through Momma's flesh, pushing back her muscle, until one day she noticed it protruding from her collarbone, poking out like a buried stone from under slippery mud.

It was Palm Sunday, and Momma was listening intently to Pastor Green's musing about how Jesus' life so closely resembled that of us everyday people—conceived out of wedlock, denied distinction, persecuted. Pastor Green went on to conclude that it is only when we follow the example of Jesus and employ an unwavering faith that we are able to rise again. It was then that Momma, dabbing her perspiring upper chest, first felt the bullet.

On Good Friday Momma lay naked from the waist up across a paper-sheet-covered table in her doctor's cold office. She closed her eyes tightly as the surgeon sliced a thin razor slit in her skin. No stitches or anesthesia were required, just a little bandage to absorb the blood after the bullet popped out. The next day Jack came to town for a visit.

Over the years I'd come to see my father the way Jesus must have seen King Herod, the faceless man who publicly professed his love for me while in secret he tried to kill off my spirit. I needed two fingers to tally my visits with Jack since he'd pierced Momma's chest, hands, and neck with his .22 pistol. There was the time he'd brought me a rabbit coat I was afraid to wear and the jar of quarters I didn't need. He had also shown up for Christmas once; instead of a shiny new toy, he clutched an envelope containing wrinkled five-dollar bills.

My image of Jack was of him paying me not to notice Momma's blood on his hands. But Momma, being one of those Jesus lovers herself, embraced that whole notion of forgive and forget, so when Jack suggested, hope spilling from his eyes, that we "put it all behind us and sit down to the table as friends," Momma obliged.

This was all agreed upon without my consent, so I felt betrayed by Momma on that night before Easter Sunday, no less, sitting at a candlelit table in the Cypress Inn Restaurant breaking bread with both my parents. To innocent observers, I'm sure we appeared to be quite the happy family—Jack ordering for all of us, then brushing his ring hand across the silk blouse framing Momma's collarbone. Aunt Patty nodded at every stupid thing that was said, while I fumbled with my napkin under the table and tried to ignore their useless chatter. Momma told Jack her plans to replace some of the shrubbery in our front yard. Jack asked Momma if she remembered the drives they used to take in his old blue Cutlass. Momma responded light-heartedly, "It was always so hot inside there." It was as though her memory had escaped from her head, the hurt drawn from her chest along with that bullet the day before.

I cracked my crab legs in silence while Momma shared her plans for the future—of getting a new car and finishing college—and Jack reminisced. The few times Jack tried to engage me in conversation, I mumbled something incoherently, never moving my eyes from the window, where I watched the moon rise along the river. Eventually, he took the hint and stopped talking to me, but my quiet triumph wouldn't last long.

Since Jack was just "passing through" on this visit, Momma acquiesced to his request that I accompany him and Aunt Patty on the drive home. The riverfront restaurant where we ate was quite a ways from Stoner Hill, so I found myself dozing in the car. Jack's bristling voice awoke me, and I listened to him with closed eyes.

"That woman ain't doing no kind of raising of my daughter," he said to Aunt Patty in an angry hush, as though he knew how to raise anything beyond expectations. I remained still but felt the glare of headlights on us as Jack went on in his flash of fury. "Yolanda don't have no respect for me. Who told her to call me Jack? That's nobody but her momma filling her head against me." I was puzzled. How had Momma found peace with this man?

Jack's words were still with me Easter morning as I watched the little girls in chiffon dresses whisper into a microphone, "Happy Easter, everybody," and sing "He Arose." Above their heads, a white paper banner glittered with the words RESUR-RECTION SUNDAY in cursive silver letters. A banquet of white, red, and yellow carnations covered the devotional table along with a plate of bread and a pewter goblet filled with wine. Large palm leaves and white bows accented each pew.

After the last Easter speech was delivered, the spotlight turned on the pulpit draped in purple. Pastor Green left his chair and stepped down before us, his red stole hanging like a valance over his white robe. Our minister began explaining Jesus' death on the cross—the rush of blood leaving his veins, the hallucinations, and his last breath.

"But there are other ways we're crucified. Cruel words, mistreatment, and abuse kill us off little by little," he said, before remarking on how difficult it is to revive a dead spirit. But if Jesus could rise from the dead, surely we can, Pastor Green assured us. "But we must carry a light heart," he pronounced, beseeching us to free ourselves from the guilt, shame, and anger that threaten to destroy us. I looked around the church to ensure that no one was looking at me, then dropped my head.

The melody of an old hymn rang from the organ, and the deaconesses stood in a row of white dresses and prepared to serve Communion. Their husbands pulled on white cotton gloves and carried silver trays holding miniature glasses and cracker crumbs to each of the parishioners. When every baptized soul held a glass of wine, Pastor instructed us. "Take this with a pure heart in remembrance of our Savior." My lips never touched the rim of the glass that day. I knew that my heart wasn't pure like Momma's. Mine was weighed down by my grudge against my father.

That May Pappy and Honeymoon took the entire family to Ralph and Kacoo's, that fancy restaurant Jack had wanted to bring me to. We were celebrating Ruby's high school graduation, and the gathering reminded me of my first memory of us all together, at Honeymoon's house for Ruby's eighth birthday. At that occasion too Big Momma had been seated in the middle of a long narrow table, with Honeymoon and Momma at her sides. Ruby's older brothers, Michael and Donny, had wrapped our eyes with blindfolds as the little kids played Pin the Tail on the Donkey. All my uncles were home, and the roar of their laughter shook the windowpanes. In the years between Uncle Rat dying and Uncle Will going to jail, the sons' laughter had quieted. Baby Jane raised his hand in a toast to his baby sister, who was headed for Louisiana Tech. Next Uncle Wayne stood up and presented Ruby with a brick, saying it was the only thing he could find harder than her head.

From there conversations passed around the table like baskets of bread. Donny told me that on the plane ride from his Air Force station in Germany he'd read an article that reminded him of the times we'd climbed the levee surrounding Stoner Hill. With some reservation (sometimes my uncle could go on endlessly), I asked him how so.

"Some college did this study on perception, right? It found that a hill is always perceived by its climber to be steeper than it actually is for the simple fact that the tireder he gets, the higher he thinks the hill is." That was always my problem climbing the levee. I'd whine the entire way up about how steep it was, but once we were settled at the top, with the breeze relaxing us, I'd always look back down that levee and say the climb hadn't been that bad at all.

Baby Jane and Uncle Wayne, an ashtray between them, shook their heads at us. I smiled toward their wives and Momma assisting the children and leaned over and asked Donny if he'd taken a trip to Paris yet.

"A couple times," he said. "The city looks like it's made of gold, but there's nowhere to park a car or plant a tree."

"Things are never what we think they'll be, huh?" I asked him, and Donny said that sometimes they're better and reminded me of how good my handpicked strawberries had tasted to me.

"The trick to climbing the hill," he explained, "is to not look too far behind you or too far up ahead for the simple fact that you want to just focus on planting your next step firmly on the ground."

The rest of the dinner went on with others offering advice to Ruby. "Keep your money hidden in your sock drawer." "Don't schedule any classes before ten in the morning." And "Attend the Rocky Valley Baptist Church." Donny's words stayed with me.

At the close of the evening, Pappy, who'd had more than one shot of bourbon, stood up and shouted down the table to Ruby, "Now, baby, there ain't nothing that we won't help you do. We might not know how to help, we might not really be able to help, but we gon' help you anyhow. There's enough of us here to make a whole anything. Right?"

"Right, right, right," came the chorus. Then Pappy picked up his worn fedora that had been resting beside him upside down on the floor. From his back pocket he took a large wad of money and dropped it in that silk-lined hat, then passed it around the table. Ruby and I watched like wide-eyed squirrels as the hat was filled with fifties, twenties, fives, and ones. Steam rose from my bowl of gumbo, bills fell to the floor, and I thanked God for such a rich family and anticipated my turn.

Clearing out my locker at school the next day, I kept thinking about the hills I'd climbed—up along the river with Uncle Donny and Ruby, over Youree Drive with Big Momma to church, to the top of the driveway with Momma behind the wheel of our old white Impala. In the past I'd done all of my climbing with a companion, but as I debated with my friends about where we should go for high school, I worried about the day I'd come to start walking alone.

Byrd High was where everyone had gone since Uncle Wayne's class had integrated the school a few years earlier. Since then the curriculum and teaching-talent pools had gotten weaker and weaker as white parents pulled their children from the rosters and sent them to private schools. Our parents couldn't afford private-school tuition, but black students could attend a school outside of their district by petitioning the school board.

On the last day of school the five of us ate together in the cafeteria the way we had in elementary school. Fizz and I faced Teresa and Dwight, who could not stop giving each other blushing side glances. Jason sat by himself at the table's end, eating everyone's leftovers. When the conversation drifted from our dull summer plans, I suggested that instead of going to Byrd, we all could go to Captain Shreve High School.

Looking squarely at Teresa, with her skin as smooth and dark as an eight ball and a mind as accurate as a well-directed pool stick, I said, "Ask yourselves, how many kids from Stoner Hill has Byrd sent to college?"

Teresa untangled her long fingers from Dwight's stout ones and pressed her fingertips against the table's edge. Staring back at me, she took her shot: "I'm not going to college."

The words landed between my eyes. It was true that we'd never talked about going to college, but I'd just assumed that she was thinking what I was thinking. After all, she'd been one of the quickest girls in our elementary school class. If Teresa wasn't going, why should I?

"I'm going to the military," she continued. She wanted to sound defiant, but it was defeat that rose and cracked in her voice like a shattering plate. And with that sound something inside me fell. Teresa couldn't let herself want to go to college. She considered herself spoiled—she always got what she wanted, but I knew well that she was careful to only want small things. She hadn't seen anyone go to college, and it was enough for her parents to get the bills paid by the end of the month. Now I was challenging her to want something bigger than she saw. I was going to challenge them all. I was trying desperately to figure out why my friends who I'd done and shared everything with didn't want to walk in my direction.

"What if we're not popular?" Teresa asked me. "What if we can't do the work?"

I had no answers. I turned to Fizz, who, having handed Jason the uneaten half of her tuna sandwich, was applying lip gloss. I decided not to even bother with the two of them, so chummy together. Maybe if I had been a part of a couple or had Fizz's looks to fall back on or could find comfort in one of Jason's joints, I would have been able to go along with them. Instead, like going to church on Sundays, this was something I'd have to do separately.

The day before beginning ninth grade, I sat on the front porch sipping orange juice and helping Big Momma peel pears to make preserves. Between us, on the hickory-wood bench carved by her brother, was a ten-gallon pot. Looking up from her knife, Big Momma asked me what I'd learned at Baptist Youth-En-Camp the week earlier.

I told her about the horny couples and about Reverend Frank's words that came to rest like a scarf over my head and shoulders. "The day you can look in the mirror and say to yourself, 'Yesterday I did the best I could and today I'll do better than that' is the day you'll see beauty in your eyes."

Big Momma knew that I didn't go about my life intending to do the best I could. So biting into a pear slice she said, "That's a tall order right there."

What she didn't know was what stopped me. It seemed to me that my family had set out to do their best but failed—Momma and Uncle Rat in their marriages, Baby Jane in college, Uncle Will in life. "Sometimes I wonder if it's worth trying. What if we never get it right?" I asked Big Momma.

She shook her head and said, "What if, what if. It's all God's plan anyway."

I waited for more, then, peeling several more pears, realized that that was all Big Momma had to say on the subject. How could she just leave it at that? Why would God want Momma lying in her own blood, Uncle Rat dead, and a child resenting her daddy?

"That's not what I mean, girl," Big Momma scolded me when I questioned her. "When you reach a place in your faith where you can believe even when the worst thing happens that God is gon' get you through it, you'll be able to see your way to the other end. When you get there, you'll be stronger and wiser for it."

I hunched my shoulders, disbelieving.

"Smell this, Londa." Big Momma held a ripe pear out to me. I took it in my hands and breathed in its sweetness. "Now, what does it taste like?" she asked. Before I could bite into the soft, heavy fruit, she stopped me. "Don't you know what it taste like already?"

"Yeah," I said, in the wary way I usually reserved for Donny.

"How you know?" Big Momma pressed. "You know 'cause you've bitten into thousands of pears before and none ever tasted like a strawberry, a fig, or a watermelon. They all tasted like a pear." Just when I was beginning to wonder if Big Momma's mind was starting to fail, she added, "Just like I know, no matter what happens, God's gon' see me to the other side of it. See, Londa," she said, carving a wedge from my pear and placing it in my mouth, "you haven't lived long enough to come out the other side of anything. But when you get to be your momma's age or, Lord have mercy, my age, you know whatever happens, God's gon' see you through." Big Momma told me she'd lived through a lot of bad things, horrible things. She remembered when she used to have to drop her eyes when a white person passed. "Now I can tell 'em to go to hell if I want," she stated frankly. She'd had her newborn die in her arms, her oldest grandson killed in his sleep, sickness tear her body down, but she said just like I know what that pear tasted like, she knew she could live through bad times and have joy at the end of the day. "That's faith, girl."

I took another bite of my pear and chewed on Big Momma's words. We sat in silence. She went back to peeling. I stared out at the lush forest, the pale green branches waving at the birds nesting, the ripe colors of pears, lemons, and sunflowers brightening the landscape, and hoped for a time when faith would rise up in me like the sun and I could be sure what the day was going to taste like.

Afterword

HONEYMOON'S GRAVEYARD JOY

> He has sent me to bind up the brokenhearted . . .
> to bestow on them a crown of beauty instead of
> ashes, the oil of gladness instead of mourning, and
> a garment of praise instead of a spirit of despair.
>
> —*Isaiah 61:1–3*

As I started the familiar drive from Washington back to Shreveport with my cousin Donna in August 1994, I had about as much intention of telling my story as a rifle-toting redneck has of being mistaken for a deer during hunting season. I was spending my days fumbling through a lopsided romance and reading other people's opinions. I was in law school at the time, being trained to put other people on the spot, but sometimes looking back is the best way to figure out where you're going.

It was my cousin who'd started me thinking about the past. Donna was fifteen the summer she lived with me in Washington. She had arrived wearing a frown, pimples, and a bra two sizes too small. She was no longer the giggly little girl who'd hung on my every word, and taking her in was like drinking spoilt milk or biting into a soft apple, that much more difficult to stomach because I'd been expecting something sweet and familiar. Her cotton polo shirt was old and her white jeans frayed at the seams, but they were clean and bright. She wanted to appear tough, but the only thing hard about her was her new pair of sand-colored Timberland ankle boots. Out of her element, she spent her first days examining my expensive-looking flea market finds and pointing out unknown faces in photographs. Where'd you get this? Who's that? she asked, acclimating herself.

My cousin was from the projects, the subsidized-housing community on the edge of Stoner Hill. Fearing that its mostly unwed residents would shelter their babies' fathers or that their weakmindedness would spill over on their already overburdened neighbors, the city had chosen to build a cage around them. Donna seemed to find this more comforting than my brick row house. I spent two months rummaging through her psyche and forbidding her from walking after dark or befriending the fast foster girl who lived next door, instead of sharing myself with her.

People often commented that we looked alike, but we differed greatly in temperament. You could see the difference in the way we approached something as benign as a movie. The week before Donna was to return home, I had taken her to see the new gangsta release, *Menace II Society*. When we arrived to find a crowd ahead of us, Donna said cynically, "Great, a line." I replied that it must be a great movie.

There was a scene in which the menacing character, O-Dog, embarrasses someone at a party by pointing out his illegitimacy. The theater broke up laughing, but Donna and I remained silent, our mirth muzzled by truth. Donna's mother had not been married to my uncle Donny or the two other men with whom she had children. My cousin thought that because I carried my father's last name I didn't share her shame, but like the Southern states we passed through on our journey home—Virginia with its arrogance, stubborn South Carolina, and Louisiana at once gay and downtrodden—our experiences were similar, but we diverged in attitude.

With hundreds of miles still ahead of us, I tried to explain this to Donna, but the insolent teenager loosened her neck and threw up the angry-woman hand and said, "If you got something to say to me, write it down." But for Donna's surfing the radio for hip-hop stations and our stops at Dairy Queen, Exxon, and Wal-Mart, it was a silent ride the rest of the way to Shreveport.

Soon after we crossed the Red River, Donna's projects were visible from the highway, but I drove a few blocks past them to our grandmother's house.

"What we doin' here?" Donna asked. I smiled and told her I wanted to give her something.

We found Honeymoon resting on the porch, having just come back from a walk. Her body, built like an upside-down pear, leaned forward as she caught her breath.

"Come on in here, girls. I got something for you," came her familiar greeting. She opened the front door with a key that hung from a bracelet made from a pair of stocking remains. As we entered the house, her poodle, Prancer, shook his chain and yelped at being kept away from the new activity. In the living room, my head bumped a blue birdcage made of Styrofoam and synthetic feathers. Honeymoon placed okra and fried liver on the mismatched plates she'd bought for ninety-nine cents with a Safeway Grocer purchase.

"Honeymoon, you got time to go by the graveyard?" I asked.

"I want to give Donna something over there." They were both too curious to object.

I was the only one who didn't mind taking Honeymoon to the cemetery. I liked the stories she told me there.

I approached Carver Cemetery's gates slowly, not out of respect but out of fear of busting up the car. Unlike the fluffy grass and tall tombstones that cover the beds of dead whites, our graveyard was fairly maintained but not immaculate. Instead of smooth, tarred-over paths, here were only worn, bumpy trails. I parked in the yard's center so that we could work our way around the grounds, which extend back against the woods. Marble monuments that stood erect were forbidden, so indistinguishable iron markers dotted the ground, along with large oak trees.

We first looked for Big Momma's grave, which should have been marked by two flower bushes that anchored the walkway nearby. The shrubs had been cut back, so we had to search a bit. Once we found it, Honeymoon kneeled and stuck into the dirt the silk sunflowers we'd just purchased from a nearby dollar store. She did the same at her father's grave while sharing images of him—legs crossed, a Camel dangling from his bottom lip.

Honeymoon told Donna how during the Depression, Grandpa George, hungry and drunk, had carried her in nothing but a wet diaper down the long road to his in-laws' house. Honeymoon's grandparents had always thought Grandpa George a fool, so they eagerly agreed over their wobbly hickory kitchen table to an even swap: Honeymoon for a loaf of bread.

"Still, he was my pa," Honeymoon said before calling out, "Blessed are they that mourn, for they shall inherit the earth."

We moved on to find Honeymoon's brothers, lying opposite

one another. Uncle Lange died as he had lived, fast and recklessly. A gambling man, he wagered on how he would go—at the hands of an angry drunk he'd beaten at cards, or by a bullet from the pistol of a scorned woman? It turned out to be neither. He died in his thirties of a rotten liver.

Uncle Peter had been Honeymoon's older brother. Unlike Donna and me, the two had been close in age and disposition. After years of smoking and working in a grocer freezer, my great-uncle was nipped in the throat by cancer. After surgery and chemotherapy, a recovery had been the prognosis, but before the doctors could be proven right, Uncle Peter choked on a spoonful of soup. "My ways are not your ways," Honeymoon quoted from a passage in her Bible as we passed his grave.

At the grave of her son, she bowed low enough to hear the ground. "The Lord giveth, the Lord taketh away. Blessed be the name of the Lord." She sighed before replacing the plastic poinsettias we'd left at Christmas with another batch of yellow artificial flowers. We didn't waste the old bunch, but left them at the grave of Uncle Rat's neighbor, a Vietnam veteran who nobody ever seemed to visit.

It was then that the tears started to come. Not from Honeymoon's eyes, but from Donna's. My cousin cried because Honeymoon had managed to do with our dead what she always tried to do with our family—bring them together. Honeymoon understood and rubbed Donna's back, which only made the girl cry harder.

"Now, now, Donna," Honeymoon said sternly. "This is the way things was meant to be."

"How do you know that, Honeymoon?"

" 'Cause it's God's will."

I watched Donna as she finally began to accept my gift—that of our grandmother's strength and wisdom. My cousin wanted to know how Honeymoon could smile surrounded by all of this. She wanted to know why Honeymoon wasn't angry.

"Angry?" Honeymoon repeated with a bewildered smile. "About what? What's so good and special about us that death can't knock on our door? It snuck up on Kallie Mae's house just last year. Why should I understand how it happens to my neighbor and not to myself?"

Honeymoon explained how some days things rested on her mind more than other days. On those she stayed on her knees a little longer.

"But I tell you what," Honeymoon said, waving her index finger in the air. "Most days I expect something wonderful to happen. On the days when the worst does, I just accept it. See, some people come here with the heart of a victim, but I got victory."

We started our walk back to the car with Donna and me dragging behind Honeymoon, whose mind had already turned to tomorrow's Sunday dinner.

"Londa, we need to go by the grocer. I need some more evaporated milk and eggs for a cake." Sensing that we weren't listening, she turned around and smothered us both with hugs and kisses. "What do you want me to cook for you, Donna? I think I'll make you some chicken and dumplings."

That Sunday was like all the others. Our plates were mountains of fried chicken, catfish, greens soaked in peppers topped with Honeymoon's hot-water cornbread. The table wasn't big enough to hold us all, so we too piled on top of one another. Still turning over Honeymoon's words, I looked on the walls and tables at our family remains: Big Momma's old Bible, Uncle Rat's hunting rifle, Uncle Peter's pipe. It was then that I realized I did have something to say to Donna and to girls like us, so I began to write our stories down.

Just then my grandmother took a seat next to Pappy and

someone turned on the radio. Suddenly the music of my past rang out. The DJ played the Jackson 5's "Dancing Machine," and I went over to Donna and wound her like I had when she was younger, pretending to be a robot. "Dance, Donna, dance," I said, and Honeymoon laughed, covering her face like a bashful schoolgirl. Before long, we were all dancing and singing, enjoying life among the living, keeping in our souls faith in our God, who shepherds us gently through tumultuous seas, and in our hearts the spirit of our loved ones who sleep peacefully under trees.

When I returned to Washington, I began to write in earnest, hoping I could convince young girls like my cousin that our experiences should give us perspective, not definition. I wanted Donna to gain from her trials understanding, compassion, and grace. It took five years of rewrites to dig those bones up. Every new page helped me uncover how these people churned heartache into gladness. They inspired me, and I hoped they could save Donna, who looked down at her hands every time someone asked about her upbringing. I wanted to give Donna the gift of knowing that we can have graveyard joy no matter where we live.

On Our Way to Beautiful

A FAMILY MEMOIR

Yolanda Young

A READER'S GUIDE

To print out copies of this or other Random House Reader's Guides,
visit us at www.randomhouse.com/rgg

Questions for Discussion

Yolanda Young grew up in Shreveport, where she spent her childhood playing in the hard-luck streets and shotgun shacks of the Stoner Hill neighborhood. At the core of her young life was a loving family whose enduring strength more than made up for their lack of money. When she wasn't gathering gems of wisdom from her great-grandmother Big Momma, Yolanda was collecting tales about the rest of her family and finding out what it really means to have dreams. Although dealing with life's twists and turns was a struggle, Young's family never gave up hope. From her grandmother Honeymoon, her own mother, and her uncles Wayne and Baby Jane, Yolanda learned values that gave her the confidence and resolve to dream bigger than her circumstances allowed.

1. Why does Yolanda Young use biblical epigraphs to begin each chapter? How does her life story reflect themes from the Bible?

2. Big Momma tells Yolanda everyone has to dream and that "there was no better way to feed the soul than to give someone a dream to hold." How important is it to have dreams? What kinds of dream are most important?

3. Both *The Autobiography of Miss Jane Pittman* by Ernest Gaines and *I Know Why the Caged Bird Sings* by Maya Angelou depict the lives of poor Southern girls. *On Our Way to Beautiful* represents the voice of a younger generation. How do Yolanda's experiences mirror those of the young women in Gaines's and Angelou's works? How do they differ?

4. In Chapter 9, the author uses children playing musical chairs to illustrate the happenstance nature of poor children's lives and the difficulties they face when trying to excel. What obstacles have you experienced in your life that have held you back in the same way? What makes Yolanda decide she can succeed?

5. The realities of race, class, and poverty make success hard to achieve in Stoner Hill, yet hopelessness never seems to take hold. Where do the residents of Stoner Hill draw their strength from? What kinds of success do they achieve?

6. Yolanda spent her childhood moving between different worlds—between her mother's and grandmother's homes, between church and school, and between Stoner Hill and Shreve Highland. Although Yolanda moved easily within her family circles, she found herself the odd one out in others—religious among a circle of friends who were not, a black girl in a predominantly white school. How successful was she in bridging the gap between these different worlds? How did it affect her decisions about her future?

7. Yolanda learns a good deal about life from the experiences of her family members; the resilience of her mother, un-

cles, grandparents, and great-grandmother teach her as much as her own experiences do. What lessons from their lives does she take with her? What does she reject?

8. At Broadmoor Yolanda sees the world beyond her Stoner Hill neighborhood. Being in the first group of students to integrate the white school is bittersweet, but she learns, to her surprise, that it is not as bad as she expected it to be. Yolanda's speech at her student council elections gives voice to all the hurt and hope she encountered at Broadmoor. What does she gain from attending school there? What does she lose?

9. Together Kitty, Honeymoon, and Big Momma represent three generations of a strong family. Yolanda's relationship with each woman is unique. What are the similarities and differences among them? How does each woman deal with adversity in her life?

10. In the chapter "Momma's Bullet Rising," the author uses the Last Supper to represent the shared suffering of all people. In light of this, would you say she ends the book with optimism or despair?

11. What does Yolanda Young come to understand about beauty and what does she mean by "on our way to beautiful"?